Expedition to the Unknown: Mallory and Irvine

The 1924 British Mount Everest Expedition

TYLER LONG

COPYRIGHT © 2025
TYLER LONG

All rights are reserved. No part of this book may be reproduced, distributed, or transmitted in any form or by any means, including photocopying, recording, or other electronic or mechanical methods, without the prior written permission of the author, except in the case of brief quotations embodied in critical reviews and certain other noncommercial uses permitted by copyright law.

Dedication

This book is dedicated to the more than 340 men and women who lost their lives on Everest. Their unwavering courage and relentless pursuit of their dreams have ignited my own aspirations, inspiring me to reach for the heights of my potential.

Contents

Dedication iii
About the Author v
Chapter One: Everest – The Third Pole and Beyond 1
Chapter Two: George Mallory – A Life Defined by Climbing 14
Chapter Three: Andrew Irvine – The Young Engineer of Everest 26
Chapter Four: The 1921 and 1922 Expeditions – Learning from Failure 38
Chapter Five: The 1924 Expedition Begins – Assembling the Dream Team 54
Chapter Six: Into the Death Zone – Mallory and Irvine's Summit Attempt 87
Chapter Seven: Disappearance and Death – Theories and Speculation 102
Chapter Eight: The Discovery of Mallory's Body in 1999 127
Chapter Nine: The Search for Andrew Irvine 143
Chapter Ten: The Legacy of Mallory and Irvine – Mountaineering's Greatest Mystery 156
References 174

About the Author

Tyler Long is a lifelong resident of Berkeley County, West Virginia, whose dedication to education and student success has shaped his career. A graduate of Hedgesville High School (1997) and Shepherd University (2002), Tyler pursued a path in education that has spanned over two decades.

He began his teaching career in the summer of 2003 at Tuscarora Elementary School in Berkeley County, working with students with behavioral disorders until 2007. From 2007 to 2011, he shifted his focus to supporting students with learning disabilities, further strengthening his commitment to inclusive education.

In 2012, Tyler transitioned into school administration, serving as Assistant Principal at Berkeley Heights Elementary for four years. In 2016, he returned to Tuscarora Elementary as Principal, where he continued to advocate for student achievement, parental involvement, and community engagement. His leadership journey reached a new milestone in 2023 when he became the Project Manager of the C.A.R.E.S. Academy, the state's premier school dedicated to supporting students with behavioral challenges.

Beyond his work in education, Tyler is also a published author. He wrote *WIRES*, a children's book released in February 2009, followed by *Three Strikes, You're Out* in 2012. His writing reflects his passion for storytelling and his belief in the power of literature to inspire young minds.

Tyler remains committed to fostering strong connections between students, parents, and the broader community. His work continues to center on ensuring that every child has the support, encouragement, and resources needed to succeed in both school and life.

Education & Credentials

- B.S., Political Science – Shepherd University, 2002
- M.A., Special Education (Multi-Categorical) – West Virginia University, 2006
- Certification, Educational Leadership – West Virginia University, 2007
- Ed.D., Educational Leadership – Shenandoah University, 2012

Chapter One:
Everest – The Third Pole and Beyond

At the dawn of the 20th century, as the world's frontiers were being defined and mapped, explorers and nations alike focused on reaching Earth's most remote and formidable destinations. The North and South Poles had been successfully conquered – Robert Peary famously reached the North Pole in 1909, and Roald Amundsen claimed victory at the South Pole in 1911. With the polar extremes now within human reach, the towering peak of Mount Everest presented itself as the next great unknown. Standing as the highest point on Earth, Everest was dubbed the "Third Pole," owing not only to its formidable height but also to its massive glaciated snowfields, which held more frozen water than anywhere on Earth outside the Polar Regions. The British, keenly aware of their position in the era's competitive global exploration, turned their sights toward Everest with fervor. Having watched American and Norwegian explorers achieve the polar victories, British ambitions aimed high – Everest, or

Peak XV, as it was known before its renaming, was to become the jewel in Britain's crown of achievements.

Climbing mountains is an endeavor that has fascinated humanity for thousands of years. Historically, people climbed mountains for practical reasons: seeking routes through treacherous ranges, finding grazing land for their animals, or searching for precious minerals like gold, silver, and iron. Yet, mountain climbing has always had a symbolic allure, representing a quest or the drive to conquer a seemingly insurmountable obstacle. This sentiment was encapsulated by George Mallory, who famously declared, "One must conquer, achieve, get to the top; one must know the end to be convinced that one can win the end."

By the 1800s, mountaineering as a sport began to take root, driven by a spirit of adventure, recognition, and the pursuit of personal fulfillment. In 1857, the Alpine Club was formed in England, heralding a new era for the activity. Initially composed of English gentlemen and focused on the Alps, the club symbolized mountaineering as an exclusive pursuit of the well-to-do. However, as the decades progressed, climbing grew beyond its elite origins, gradually becoming accessible to people of all ages, genders, and walks of life.

This evolution paralleled a broader shift in the world of exploration, where achievements were celebrated not only for their practical implications but also for the glory and recognition they brought to individuals and nations. Mountaineering epitomized this shift, with climbers charting their successes and setting sights on the peaks that remained unconquered. By the early 20th century, many of the world's most iconic mountains, save Everest, had been summited. This set the stage for Everest to emerge as the ultimate symbol of human ambition and endurance, challenging explorers to push beyond their limits and reach the highest point on Earth.

The task, however, was far from straightforward. Everest was, and remains, a realm of extreme danger. Its immense scale, coupled with its treacherous climate and geography, tested every facet of human endurance and skill. In 1924, it was this powerful allure of the unknown that spurred George Mallory and Andrew "Sandy" Irvine to risk their lives on the slopes of Everest, hoping to claim the summit and cement Britain's place in exploration history.[1]

The early 20th century was an age marked by exploration "fever," a period driven by both national pride and a deep-seated curiosity about Earth's most isolated and challenging locations. As expeditions

---

[1] (The Guardian) Heroism, Sacrifice, Defeat? The enduring mystery of George Mallory's final Everest Attempt

ventured into unmapped deserts and river systems across the Amazon and Africa, Everest stood as one of the last great unexplored natural wonders. For explorers like Mallory and Irvine, reaching its summit was more than a scientific endeavor; it represented the fulfillment of human potential and the unyielding pursuit of discovery.

The polar conquests, in particular, redefined what humanity considered achievable. However, unlike the Arctic or Antarctic, Everest presented an even greater challenge – not only because of its height and environmental extremes but due to the spiritual, cultural, and geographical barriers it represented. As explorers shifted their attention to the Third Pole, they were met with the unforgiving nature of high-altitude mountaineering, a discipline still in its infancy. There were no precedents or established techniques for scaling a mountain of this magnitude, which only served to increase its allure.

The motivations driving explorers like Mallory and Irvine were manifold. For Mallory, climbing Everest was both an exploration and a quest for personal meaning. When asked why he wanted to climb the mountain, he famously responded, "Because it's there." This sentiment captured the era's sense of adventure and the desire to push beyond known limits. Irvine, though younger and less experienced, shared this ambition and brought technical knowledge that would prove essential for the expedition's use of early oxygen equipment.

For the British, Everest was also a matter of national prestige. The defeat of other polar pursuits left Everest as a chance to reclaim the spotlight and showcase British endurance and tenacity. The 1924 expedition, though a dangerous gamble, was as much a point of honor as a scientific exploration.

Mount Everest, towering at a staggering 29,031 feet (8,848 meters), rises from the heart of the Himalayan mountain range, which spans over 2,400 kilometers through parts of India, Nepal, China, Bhutan, and Pakistan. The collision of the Indian and Eurasian tectonic plates some 50 million years ago formed this range, creating a jagged spine of peaks that includes the world's tallest. Everest straddles the border between Nepal and Tibet, with its southern slopes in Nepal and northern face in Tibet. This geographic positioning creates a mountain that is both geographically imposing and culturally significant.

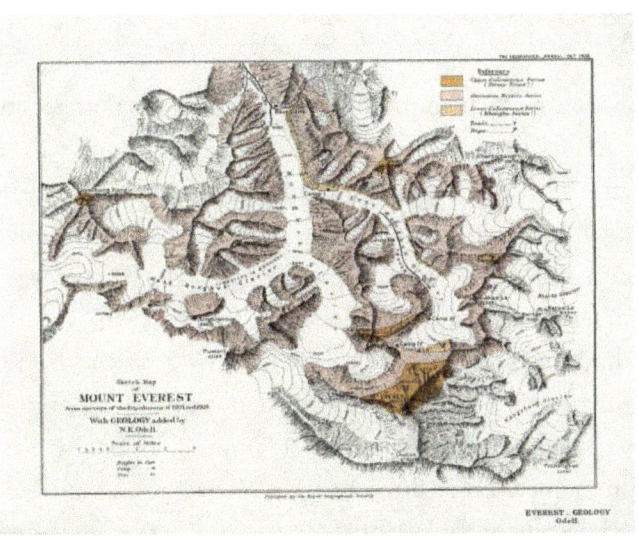

To the people of Nepal, the mountain is known as "Sagarmatha," meaning "Goddess of the Sky." To the Tibetan Sherpas, it is "Chomolungma," or "Goddess Mother of the World."² These names reflect the deep reverence that locals hold for Everest. Climbing it was not only a physical challenge but a spiritual journey that required a deep respect for the mountain's sacred status. The Sherpa people, who

---

² [(MSU) The Naming of Mount Everest](#)

have lived in the region for centuries, view the mountain as a deity, demanding both respect and humility from all who ascend it. For the early British climbers, this cultural context added a unique layer of complexity, as they learned to navigate both the mountain's physical and spiritual landscapes.

The mountain's naming history reflects the evolution of its discovery and measurement. Initially designated as "Gamma," it was renamed "Peak b" in 1847 when surveyors suspected it might surpass Kangchenjunga, then believed to be the world's highest peak. As more measurements were conducted, the mountain's exceptional height became clear, leading to another designation as "Peak XV."

In 1856, after years of meticulous calculations that accounted for light refraction, barometric pressure, temperature, and tidal data, the British officially declared Peak XV's height to be 29,002 feet (8,839.8 meters). In his Report No. 29B, paragraph 9, Andrew Waugh proposed naming the peak "Mont Everest" after Sir George Everest, who had served as Surveyor General of India from 1830 to 1843. Everest had revolutionized India's surveying methods during his tenure, introducing the most advanced and precise techniques of the time. Notably, Sir George Everest himself opposed having the mountain named after him, but the Royal Geographical Society proceeded despite his objections.

Mountaineering in the 1920s was an endeavor of almost unimaginable difficulty, requiring a combination of physical resilience, psychological fortitude, and technical skill that few possessed. Climbers like Mallory and Irvine faced a host of challenges on Everest, starting with extreme cold that could reach -30 to -40 degrees Celsius. Winds howled across the slopes, frequently exceeding 100 miles per hour, particularly in winter. This relentless wind, known as the "Jet Stream," posed a constant threat, bringing life-threatening wind chills and making movement nearly impossible at times.

Adding to the climbers' peril was the thin atmosphere at Everest's altitude. At the summit, the air pressure is about one-third of that at sea level, making oxygen a scarce resource. Altitude sickness, a severe condition that can cause confusion, loss of consciousness, and even death, is common on Everest, and the rudimentary oxygen tanks available to Mallory and Irvine were prone to malfunction. According to Melanie Windridge in a Forbes article on mountaineering clothing, their equipment, while state-of-the-art for 1924, was hardly sufficient by today's standards. This assessment was confirmed when George Mallory's body was discovered in 1999, providing crucial insights into the expedition's preparation against Everest's brutal conditions through his remarkably preserved clothing inventory.[3]

His layered ensemble included, for the lower body, white thermal long underwear beneath brown medium-weave wool long johns, complemented by light brown wool leggings (known as puttees) and wool knickers. His upper body protection consisted of white wool long underwear, a faded light green silk button-down shirt bearing the label "Junior Army & Navy Stores," a blue and white pinstripe flannel shirt, and a thick-weave brown wool jumper (sweater). The outer layer was a state-of-the-art Burberry windproof climbing suit made of lightweight gabardine – an army green, tight-weave cotton shell jacket with pockets and buttons. For his extremities, Mallory wore both green fingerless wool knit gloves and fur-lined leather gloves, three pairs of medium-weave wool socks inside hobnail boots (notably without inner boots), and a fur-lined leather bomber hat for head

---

[3] (Forbes) Everest 100 Years Ago – Clothing Myths And How Outdoor Clothing Has Evolved

protection. This layering system, while innovative for its time, offered limited protection against the mountain's extreme conditions.

The geological obstacles posed by the mountain further compounded the risks. Everest's terrain is a series of glaciers, crevasses, ice towers known as seracs, and shifting snow bridges. These formations create deadly traps that could give way without warning, swallowing climbers into depths from which rescue was virtually impossible. The Khumbu Glacier, with its icefall riddled with hidden crevasses and towering ice blocks, was one of the first obstacles facing the climbers.

The 1924 expedition faced treacherous conditions without the safety measures common in modern climbing. Above the South Col, unlike today's expeditions, which utilize fixed ropes and ladders, these early climbers had to traverse dangerous terrain with only basic equipment, transforming each step into a potential life-or-death decision. The ever-present threat of avalanches cast a dark shadow over their endeavor, made all the more poignant by recent tragedy – just two years earlier, during the 1922 expedition, seven Sherpas had lost their lives in a devastating avalanche. This tragic event, part of Everest's long history with avalanches that has claimed at least 22 lives, served as a sobering reminder of the mountain's lethal power for the 1924 team.

Expedition To The Unknown: Mallory And Irvine

While the physical dangers of Everest were immense, the spiritual significance of the mountain imposed its own demands. For the Sherpa people, each ascent of Chomolungma was not simply an act of climbing but a journey that required spiritual preparation and respect. British climbers, like those of the 1924 expedition, were introduced to these beliefs through interactions with local guides and porters, many of whom saw their work on the mountain as a sacred duty, connecting them with their deity. This sense of reverence demanded a cautious approach to the climb, imbuing each step with a degree of humility in the face of the immense power of nature.

The British explorers encountered local customs that added layers of meaning to their climb. Rituals to appease the mountain spirits were commonplace, and before expeditions, climbers would sometimes seek blessings from local lamas or shamans. Such customs created a sense of shared purpose between the British climbers and their Sherpa guides, uniting them in a common, albeit perilous, mission.

The climate on Everest was and is notorious. In addition to the freezing temperatures and fierce winds, the 1924 expedition faced unpredictable weather that could shift rapidly, bringing sudden storms. Noel Odell, a member of the British team and the last person to see Mallory and Irvine alive, later recounted that a blizzard swept over the mountain on the day they disappeared, potentially sealing their fate.[4]

Everest's geology presented further obstacles. Its rock layers, twisted by tectonic forces, created vertical cliffs and unstable ridges. The Three Steps are a series of prominent rocky formations located on the northeast ridge of Mount Everest. These features, situated at extreme altitudes of 28,097 feet, 28,250 feet, and 28,580 feet, pose significant challenges to climbers ascending the mountain via the standard north route. Each of these steps represents a formidable obstacle due to their technical difficulty and their location within the Death Zone, where extreme altitude severely compromises physical and cognitive performance.

The First Step, positioned at 28,097 feet, comprises a series of large, uneven boulders. Despite being the lowest of the three, this step remains a significant hurdle even for seasoned climbers. The combination of technical climbing demands, exposure to high winds, and the physiological toll of extreme altitude has claimed the lives of

---

[4] (BBC) Everest pioneers 'hit by storm'

numerous mountaineers in this section. Its location deep within the Death Zone amplifies the dangers, as climbers are more vulnerable to exhaustion and hypoxia while attempting to traverse the precarious terrain.

The Second Step, located at an altitude of 28,250 feet, is widely regarded as the most challenging and historically significant of the three. This section features a nearly vertical climb of approximately 130 feet, with the final five feet being almost entirely vertical. The step gained prominence during the 1960 Chinese expedition, when climbers Wang Fuzhou, Gongbu, and Qu Yinhua claimed to have successfully surmounted the obstacle, reportedly using their teammate Liu Lianman as a human ladder. While their ascent is generally recognized, the lack of photographic or physical evidence has left some aspects of the claim unresolved in mountaineering circles.

In 1975, a Chinese team permanently altered the Second Step by installing a 15-foot aluminum ladder to assist climbers in overcoming the near-vertical section. This modification significantly reduced the technical difficulty of the climb, making it more accessible to subsequent expeditions. In 2007, the original ladder was replaced with a newer one by a collaborative effort between Chinese and international teams, further enhancing climbers' safety while navigating this critical segment.

The Third Step, at an altitude of 28,580 feet, is the smallest and least technically demanding of the three. With a climbing height of approximately 33 feet, it serves as the final rocky barrier before climbers reach the summit snowfield. While not as formidable as the previous two steps, the Third Step still requires caution, as even minor missteps at such altitudes can prove fatal.

The "Hillary Step," located on the southeast ridge of Mount Everest, was a nearly vertical rock face and one of the final challenges climbers faced before reaching the summit. Situated halfway between the South Summit and the True Summit, at an elevation of 28,839 feet above sea level, the step was a 40-foot vertical obstacle that required immense technical skill and physical endurance to overcome. It gained historical significance in 1953 when Sir Edmund Hillary and Tenzing Norgay became the first climbers to successfully reach Everest's summit, with Hillary famously shimmying up this formidable feature.

While the Hillary Step became synonymous with Everest's southeast ridge route, it is important to note that it lies on a different side of the mountain than the route attempted by Mallory and Irvine in 1924, who climbed via the North Col and Northeast Ridge. Nevertheless, the Hillary Step stood as a symbol of the challenges Everest presents, irrespective of the path chosen.

The 2015 earthquake, which devastated much of the Everest region, significantly altered this iconic landmark. How extensive was the damage? Experts continue to study its impact, yet leading mountaineers offer differing perspectives. Kenton Cool, the world-renowned climber who has summited Everest 18 times, reports that the Hillary Step is now only 12 to 15 feet high. Others, like Tim Mosedale, asserted in 2017 that the Hillary Step has collapsed entirely. Mosedale noted, "The chunk of rock named 'The Hillary Step' is definitely not there anymore."

This alteration may render Everest an even more dangerous climb, as the collapse of the Hillary Step eliminates one of its most recognizable and formidable barriers while introducing new, unpredictable challenges for climbers attempting the southeast ridge.

The 1924 British Mount Everest expedition embodied the spirit of an age determined to push the boundaries of human endeavor. For Mallory, Irvine, and their peers, Everest represented the ultimate test – a challenge that called for courage, resilience, and a willingness to confront both the known and the unknown. Their journey up the mountain was not only a quest for glory but also a confrontation with nature at its most unforgiving. Although Mallory and Irvine's fate remains a mystery, their attempt marked a profound moment in the history of exploration, inspiring future generations to take up the mantle and, in time, conquer Everest.

Chapter Two:
George Mallory – A Life Defined by Climbing

George Herbert Leigh Mallory was born on June 18, 1886, to Herbert Leigh Mallory and Annie Beridge in Mobberley, Cheshire, England. His birthplace, Newton Hall, was a classic English country estate where he spent his earliest years. The Mallory family, deeply rooted in the Anglican tradition, emphasized discipline, intellectual curiosity, and respect for nature. George, along with his two sisters, Mary Henrietta (known as Avie) and Annie Victoria, and his younger brother, Trafford, inherited a love for exploration and adventure from an early age. George's parents noted his fearless nature, and his sister Avie famously recalled, "He climbed everything that it was at all possible to climb." From scaling his father's church at age seven to ascending every climbable surface within reach, young George's life seemed predestined for heights.

As the family moved from Newton Hall to Hobcroft House, Mobberley, George's early adventures began taking form. He often tested his balance and agility by climbing up and down the home's draperies and scrambling over rooftops. These early climbs were the first steps on a journey that would eventually place him on the world's highest mountain. His natural affinity for climbing grew in parallel with his intellectual curiosity, a combination that would define him as both a mountaineer and a thinker.

Mallory's formal education began at Glengorse Boarding School in Eastbourne, where his potential in academics became clear. His academic journey took a pivotal turn in 1900 when he won a Mathematics Scholarship to attend Winchester College, one of England's most prestigious public schools. Winchester's rigorous curriculum and emphasis on both academic and physical prowess provided an ideal environment for Mallory to cultivate his love for literature, philosophy, and the outdoors. In addition to his intellectual pursuits, Mallory excelled as an athlete, becoming the school's best gymnast, particularly skilled on the parallel bars. He was also a member of the school's rifle team, demonstrating physical prowess and precision – qualities that would later prove essential in his mountaineering pursuits.

It was at Winchester that Mallory encountered Robert Lock Graham Irving, a housemaster who would profoundly influence his future. Irving, an accomplished mountaineer and member of the Alpine Club, was renowned for his advocacy of solitary climbing. Recognizing Mallory's potential, Irving introduced him to the discipline and art of mountaineering. Eager to impart his love for the mountains, Irving took Mallory and his classmate Harry Gibson on an expedition to the Alps in August 1904. This trip marked Mallory's first experience with high-altitude climbing, though it came with challenges. The group's initial attempt to summit Mont Velan ended 600 feet below the peak, as both Mallory and Gibson were struck by altitude sickness. However, the expedition continued with notable successes, including the summits of Dufourspitze on August 13 and Mont Blanc on August 26, marking the beginning of Mallory's lifelong dedication to mountain climbing.

From 1905 to 1913, Mallory refined his skills across England, Wales, Scotland, and the Alps. His climbing journey through these regions exposed him to various challenges that would sharpen his abilities and prepare him for Everest's extreme conditions. In England, particularly in the Lake District, he climbed with a group of skilled mountaineers, including notable figures like Geoffrey Winthrop Young and Siegfried Herford. Together, they attempted routes like those on Pillar Rock and Scafell. "Mallory's Route" on Pillar Rock, known for its hard 5a grade, mirrored the technical difficulty of Everest's infamous Second Step, pushing him to develop advanced climbing techniques that would later prove essential.

Mallory also found challenging terrain in Wales, particularly in Snowdonia, where he often trained on rugged peaks like Snowdon, the highest point in Wales. Snowdonia's sheer cliffs and rocky terrain provided an ideal testing ground for Mallory's climbing style, which emphasized both speed and technique. These Welsh peaks forced him to rely on precision and agility, elements that became signature aspects of his climbing approach.

In Scotland, Mallory encountered even harsher conditions, particularly during winter ascents. One of his significant early accomplishments was scaling Ben Nevis, the tallest peak in the British Isles, on April 6, 1906, alongside Irving and Guy Leach. The trio also summited Stob Ban and Càrn Mòr Dearg, navigating icy slopes and mixed precipitation. These Scottish climbs further honed Mallory's skill set, making him physically tougher and better prepared for the brutal conditions he would later face in the Himalayas.

Yet it was the Alps that offered Mallory his most rigorous training grounds. Between 1909 and 1913, he repeatedly returned to the region, challenging himself on high-altitude peaks like Mont Blanc, the Aiguille du Grépon, and the Dent du Géant. Here, he not only adapted to climbing at significant elevations but also navigated the complex snow and ice environments characteristic of alpine terrain. These Alpine adventures, undertaken with climbers like Irving, Gibson, Harry Tyndale, Harold Porter, and Hugh Pope, refined his techniques in a way that the British mountains could not. In these peaks, Mallory gained valuable experience with crevasse navigation, ropework, and acclimatization – skills he would later depend on during his expeditions to the Himalayas.

In 1913, Mallory's life took a new direction when he met Ruth Turner at a dinner held by Arthur Clutton-Brock. The two shared a love for literature, art, and the outdoors, forming an intellectual and emotional bond that quickly deepened. Ruth, the daughter of Hugh Thackeray Turner, a prominent architect, was both cultured and well-educated. Her outlook complemented Mallory's ambitions, and their shared ideals made them kindred spirits. Following a family holiday in Venice with the Turners, Mallory and Ruth's relationship blossomed into a serious courtship.

By May 1914, they were engaged, and Ruth's family provided them with a six-bedroom home called "The Holt" in Godalming,

Surrey, as a wedding gift. They married on July 29, 1914, just days before Britain entered World War I. The wedding was officiated by Mallory's father, with Geoffrey Winthrop Young serving as his best man. Together, they began a family, eventually having three children: Frances Clare, born in 1915; Beridge Ruth, affectionately called "Berry," born in 1917; and John, born in 1920. Though Ruth deeply loved her husband, the personal risks associated with his climbing pursuits placed a strain on their relationship. Ruth supported his ambitions yet harbored concerns about the dangers he faced in the mountains. This tension between his passion for mountaineering and his responsibilities as a husband and father became an underlying struggle as he prepared for his Everest expeditions.

When World War I erupted in August 1914, Mallory, like many of his peers, felt a strong sense of duty and wished to join the British Army. Mallory tried to enlist in the service but his job as a school teacher was considered essential. As a result, he would not be released from his duties until 1915, when the headmaster at the school found a replacement for him. He enlisted as a second lieutenant in the Royal Garrison Artillery, where he was assigned to the 40th Siege Battery. Mallory's choice of artillery allowed him to avoid the close-combat dangers that infantrymen faced, although he still encountered the constant threat of trench warfare. His letters to Ruth reveal a candid perspective on the war's intensity. Describing the bombardments, he wrote: "It was very noisy... with a 60-pounder... annoying of them... its vigorous blast". In one letter from July 1916, during the Battle of the Somme, he speculated on the war's progress, showing a cautious optimism that contrasts with the darker realities he faced.

Despite avoiding direct combat, Mallory was exposed to the brutality of war, witnessing the horrors of flamethrowers and massive casualties. This experience left him psychologically scarred. In a letter from August 15, 1916, he confided to Ruth about the unsettling effects of witnessing death: "I don't object to corpses so long as they are fresh... With the wounded, it is different. It always distresses me to see them." Such remarks reveal the toll that witnessing constant death and suffering took on Mallory's mental state, shaping his worldview as he emerged from the war.

Mallory's wartime service also had a lasting physical impact. While he avoided major injuries, his duties tested his endurance under conditions not unlike those he would face on Everest: long stretches of harsh weather, limited food, and extreme fatigue. This period hardened his resilience, reinforcing the mental and physical fortitude he would need for high-altitude expeditions.

Following the Armistice in November 1918, Mallory returned to England in January 1919 and resumed his teaching career at Charterhouse School. Although he initially embraced the stability, Mallory soon found himself disenchanted with the academic life. The war had fundamentally altered his sense of purpose, leaving him restless and yearning for the freedom of the mountains. The intellectual challenges of the classroom paled in comparison to the allure of high-altitude exploration, and he increasingly turned his attention back to mountaineering. By this time, Mallory's name was well-known within Britain's climbing circles, and he was increasingly viewed as a leading figure in the field.

In January 1921, the Royal Geographical Society and the Alpine Club formally created the Mount Everest Committee, a coalition devoted to organizing a British expedition to Everest. The committee saw Mallory as an ideal candidate. His years of training, early achievements, and distinguished reputation in Britain's mountaineering circles made him uniquely qualified for the physical and psychological demands of such an ambitious project. However, the decision was not easy for Mallory. While the expedition offered a chance to reach the world's highest summit, it would mean a prolonged separation from his family and would expose him to considerable risk. Torn between his responsibilities at home and his yearning for the mountains, he hesitated.

A visit from his close friend Geoffrey Winthrop Young helped sway his decision. Young emphasized the significance of the expedition, not only for Mallory's career but also for British national pride. Eventually, Ruth gave her blessing, recognizing that this opportunity meant as much to Mallory as their shared life together. With her reluctant support, Mallory committed to joining the 1921 reconnaissance mission to Everest.

The 1921 expedition was the first organized attempt to survey Everest's terrain and assess viable routes to the summit. Departing from Tilbury Port aboard the SS Sardinia, Mallory joined a team tasked with scouting the northern face of the mountain. This expedition was not designed to reach the summit but rather to gather vital information for a future summit attempt. Over months, Mallory and his team explored the mountain's glaciers, ridges, and high-altitude conditions. For Mallory, it was an awe-inspiring experience. He later described Everest as "a prodigious white fang excrescent from the jaw of the world," conveying the majestic, intimidating presence of the peak.

The reconnaissance mission's greatest achievement was identifying the North Col, which the team believed could serve as a feasible route toward the summit. Mallory's observations of the mountain's physical obstacles, including unstable ice, severe glacial crevasses, and violent storms, underscored the significant risks that any future climbers would face. His thorough documentation became crucial for the Mount Everest Committee's planning of the next expedition, and his vivid accounts captivated the public, amplifying support for the British mission to conquer Everest.

Upon returning to Britain, Mallory embarked on a lecture tour to share his experiences. His passionate portrayal of the mountain as a place of unmatched beauty and danger captured the British imagination. The expedition not only inspired national pride but also strengthened Mallory's resolve to reach the summit. The 1921 reconnaissance gave him a tantalizing glimpse of Everest's heights, and he became increasingly determined to scale its formidable slopes.

In 1922, Mallory joined a second expedition to Everest, this time with the explicit aim of reaching the summit. This expedition marked the first serious attempt by any team to achieve the ascent, fueled by Mallory's newfound commitment and the hope generated by the reconnaissance findings. The Mount Everest Committee's preparations were extensive, focusing on improving equipment, acclimatization strategies, and the use of supplemental oxygen – an innovation for the time.

Despite the best efforts of the team, the expedition was fraught with difficulties. Severe weather conditions, altitude sickness, and logistical challenges hindered their progress. The use of supplemental oxygen proved inconsistent, with equipment failures and concerns over the physical effects of relying on it. Mallory himself was ambivalent about oxygen, viewing it as a potential aid but questioning its impact on the purity of the climb. His physical conditioning and mental resilience enabled him to lead the team through many obstacles, but as they ascended, the dangers became increasingly clear.

Expedition To The Unknown: Mallory And Irvine

A significant tragedy struck during this expedition, reinforcing the mountain's deadly reputation. An avalanche on the slopes claimed the lives of seven Sherpas, a devastating reminder of the risks involved. Mallory was deeply affected by their deaths, which left a lasting impression on him. Despite the sorrow and setbacks, Mallory and his team reached a record altitude of 26,800 feet before being forced to turn back. Though they did not reach the summit, the climb established a new high-altitude record and solidified Mallory's belief that reaching the top was achievable with the right conditions.

Following the 1922 expedition, Mallory returned to Britain with a mixture of pride and frustration. The near-success of the climb weighed heavily on him, and he felt an obligation to continue the pursuit. To secure funding for another expedition, the Mount Everest Committee organized a lecture series across Britain and North America, naming Mallory and George Finch as principal speakers. Mallory's lectures became popular events, combining vivid descriptions of his experiences with photographs and maps. These public appearances not only fueled interest in the next expedition but also helped generate essential financial support.

In early 1923, Mallory embarked on a tour across North America, where he encountered both enthusiastic audiences and logistical setbacks. While major cities like New York, Washington, and Philadelphia provided large audiences, events in other cities, particularly in Canada, were less successful. Despite these challenges, Mallory's charm and wit won over many attendees, and his now-famous response to why he wanted to climb Everest – "Because it's there" – became emblematic of the human spirit's thirst for adventure.

Privately, however, Mallory wrestled with doubts and a growing sense of internal conflict. He had re-established a life in England with

Ruth and their children, and his career at Cambridge was on a positive trajectory. The stability of family life and academic work was appealing, yet the pull of Everest remained strong. He confided in Ruth, who understood but feared for his safety. She once wrote to him, "I love you and you love me and that ought to be happiness for a lifetime together, but I do want you. I want to live together all the time and share thoughts and joys and sorrows, and we can't apart as we can together." Mallory's response revealed his own struggle: "I am having a horrible time on a tightrope. It would be an awful tug going away instead of settling down here with Ruth, but it would look rather grim to see others without me, conquering the summit."

In early 1924, the Everest Committee launched preparations for another expedition, and Mallory's name was at the forefront. He vacillated over the decision to join, frequently seeking counsel from Ruth, friends, and even his employer. Yet despite his reservations, he felt an immense responsibility to continue. For Mallory, Everest represented unfinished business. The memory of the 1922 expedition and the tantalizing proximity to the summit fueled his determination. Furthermore, he felt a duty toward the team, many of whom relied on his experience and guidance.

The decision weighed heavily on Mallory. By this time, he was one of Britain's foremost mountaineers and the public's expectations were high. As he wrestled with his choice, he also faced increasing pressure from friends and colleagues who believed he was uniquely suited to the task. Even Ruth, despite her deep concerns, recognized the importance of this endeavor to Mallory's spirit.

In April 1924, he committed once more to the expedition, which would aim to reach the summit through the North Col route. As he prepared to depart, Mallory gave one of his most reflective and poignant responses to the question of why he climbed: "The first question you will ask, which I must try to answer, is this: what is the use of climbing Mount Everest? And my answer must be it's of no use. There isn't the slightest prospect of any gain whatsoever. So if you cannot understand that there is something in man that responds to the challenge of this mountain and goes out to meet it, but the struggle is the struggle of life itself, upward and forever upward, then you won't see why we go. What we get from this adventure is sheer joy; joy is, after all, the end of life."

With those words, Mallory set off on the 1924 expedition, carrying with him the hopes of a nation, the unwavering support of his family, and his own deep-seated desire to reach the summit of Everest. He left behind a family who loved him, and in the months that followed, he would face the most challenging, and ultimately the final, climb of his life. This last journey to Everest would cement his legacy, but also end in the mystery and tragedy that continues to define George Mallory's place in mountaineering history.

Chapter Three:
Andrew Irvine – The Young Engineer of Everest

Andrew Comyn "Sandy" Irvine was born on April 8, 1902, in Birkenhead, England, to parents William and Lilian Irvine. As the youngest of six children in a well-established family, Andrew enjoyed the privileges of an affluent upbringing. His father, William Irvine, was a successful civil engineer and respected historian in Liverpool, while his mother, Lilian Davies-Colley, came from an affluent background and was known for her involvement in social and charitable causes. The Irvine family's financial stability allowed for extensive travel and top-tier education for their children, including Andrew. This privileged lifestyle shaped Andrew's character, providing him with opportunities to develop his mechanical aptitude and explore a wide range of interests from a young age (Salkeld, 2000).

Despite his comfortable upbringing, Irvine's early life was not untouched by tragedy. At just 13 years old, he faced the death of his older brother Tom, who was killed in action during the Battle of Aubers Ridge in 1915. This loss, compounded by the suffering of others in his family due to the war – such as his cousin, who endured lifelong injuries from mustard gas – left a lasting impression on young Andrew. These experiences likely influenced the stoicism and adventurous spirit he would later exhibit in his life (Jones, 2001).

Andrew's early fascination with engineering and mechanics became evident in his childhood. At the age of 14, he sent plans for a gyroscopic gear that would allow a machine gun to fire through a propeller – a concept that represented a significant advance in weaponry. This ingenuity and problem-solving ability foreshadowed the technical skills that would earn him a place on the Everest expedition a decade later. His passion for tinkering and improving mechanical systems was a hallmark of his character.

In 1916, Andrew began attending Shrewsbury School, one of England's leading public schools. There, he excelled in sports, particularly rowing, boxing, and rugby, while his academic performance remained inconsistent. His struggles with subjects such as Greek and Latin, central to the curriculum, stood in contrast to his success in sciences and engineering, where his natural problem-solving abilities shone. Irvine's achievements on the river, however, were undeniable. In 1919, as part of the Shrewsbury School crew team, he participated in the Peace Regatta at Henley and secured a hard-fought victory against Bedford School in the Elsenham Cup final. His combination of physical strength and determination on the water made him a standout athlete.

Some historians have speculated that Andrew Irvine may have been dyslexic, citing his academic struggles as evidence. His brothers teasingly referred to him as "not being very bright," though they acknowledged his natural talent for methodical study and lateral thinking. Salkeld (2000) noted that Irvine's inconsistent academic results, paired with his exceptional mechanical and athletic abilities, hint at the possibility of dyslexia. Jones (2001) observed that Irvine struggled with subjects like Latin and Greek during his time at Shrewsbury School – disciplines requiring strong reading and memorization skills – yet he excelled in mathematics and engineering, which emphasize problem-solving and spatial reasoning. However, there is no formal evidence to confirm this diagnosis, as dyslexia was not a recognized condition during his lifetime, and his difficulties were likely dismissed as typical academic underperformance.

During a family summer holiday in 1919 in Llanfairfechan, a coastal village in North Wales, Irvine made an impression with his daring. While his family traveled by train, Andrew arrived in his prized possession: a Clyno motorcycle with a sidecar, showcasing his fascination with vehicles and engineering. It was on this holiday that Irvine reportedly drove his motorcycle to the summit of Foel Grach, a 3,000-foot mountain in Snowdonia, where he encountered Noel Odell, a mountaineer and future expedition partner. The two had no recollection of this meeting when they crossed paths again in 1923.

In 1921, Irvine applied to study Chemistry at Magdalen College, Oxford, but was rejected. Undeterred, he attended a crammer to improve his grades, particularly in Greek and Latin, and successfully gained admission to Merton College, Oxford, in 1922. At Oxford, Irvine thrived both academically and socially, performing well in his chemistry preliminaries and becoming a beloved member of the university community. His charisma and athleticism made him a popular figure among his peers, not just in the rowing squad but across the student body.

Irvine's time at Oxford was transformative. It was here that his passion for exploration and engineering truly flourished. He joined the Oxford University Mountaineering Club and continued rowing as part of the university crew team. His physical strength and determination earned him a spot in the prestigious 1923 Oxford and Cambridge Boat Race, a milestone that coincided with a pivotal moment in his life. It was during his rowing training that he was approached by Captain Noel Odell, a Cambridge geologist and mountaineer, who invited Irvine to join the Oxford University expedition to the Arctic later that year.

The Arctic expedition, organized by Merton alumnus George Binney, took place in the summer of 1923 and proved to be a significant experience for Irvine. The team set off from Newcastle and traveled to Tromsø, Norway, before embarking on a whaling vessel to the island of Spitsbergen. The expedition involved physically demanding survey work, navigating treacherous glacial crevasses, and climbing peaks up to 5,500 feet. Irvine's ingenuity and mechanical skills were invaluable during the expedition. He repaired equipment that had fallen into disrepair, earning the admiration of Odell, who praised his resilience and ability to handle extreme cold and discomfort. This experience not only solidified Irvine's reputation as a skilled problem solver but also prepared him for the challenges he would face on Everest.

Despite his growing interest in mountaineering, Irvine had relatively little formal climbing experience before the Everest expedition. His most notable ascent was of Napes Needle in the Lake District in 1923, a popular beginner's climb. His other climbs in Snowdonia were more akin to hiking and scrambling, which involve using both hands and feet to traverse steep, rocky terrain. This lack of high-altitude experience made Irvine's inclusion in the Everest expedition remarkable, underscoring the significance of his mechanical expertise and physical strength.

The 1924 British Everest expedition came into Irvine's life during a period of personal turmoil. While he was beginning to earn a name for himself at Oxford, he became embroiled in a scandal involving his best friend, Dick Summers, and Summers' stepmother, Marjory. Irvine, known for his charm and good looks, had allegedly engaged in an affair with Marjory, a former chorus girl and the much younger wife of steel magnate Henry Summers. The affair, which included clandestine trips in Rolls-Royces and intimate picnics, came to light when a friend of Henry Summers saw Irvine leaving Marjory's bedroom. This scandal may have influenced Irvine's decision to accept an invitation to join the Everest expedition, offering an escape from the drama in England.

On October 24, 1923, Irvine received a formal invitation from the Mount Everest Committee to join the 1924 expedition. Brigadier-General Charles Bruce, the expedition leader, described Irvine as the team's "splendid experiment," acknowledging his lack of climbing experience but emphasizing his exceptional physical condition and mechanical skills. Bruce believed Irvine's adaptability and strength would be assets to the team, while Noel Odell referred to him as their potential "Superman." Irvine's role as the expedition's Oxygen Officer underscored his technical contributions. He spent months redesigning and improving the oxygen apparatus from the 1922 expedition, reducing the equipment's weight by 11 pounds. Though his designs were ultimately rejected by the manufacturer, his dedication to refining the tools demonstrated his commitment to the mission.

By February 29, 1924, Irvine had set sail on the SS *California* with three other members of the Everest expedition. At 22 years old, he was the youngest and least experienced member of the team. Despite his inexperience, his physical prowess, mechanical aptitude, and resilience had earned him the respect of senior expedition leaders. His role as Oxygen Officer meant he was responsible for maintaining and managing the oxygen systems – equipment that many on the team believed would be vital for reaching the summit.

The weight and functionality of oxygen systems were critical factors in high-altitude climbing, and Irvine's contributions to improving the apparatus were widely acknowledged. Though Siebe Gorman & Co., the equipment manufacturers, ultimately rejected Irvine's suggested modifications, his efforts demonstrated his innovative thinking and problem-solving skills. His redesigns, which included simplifying the apparatus and reducing its weight, showed his determination to ensure the team had the best possible chance of success. His commitment to mastering the mechanics of the equipment highlighted his meticulous nature and ability to adapt to the challenges of an expedition of this scale.

When Irvine reached Darjeeling, India, in March 1924, he joined the rest of the expedition team, including George Mallory. At first, Mallory found Irvine likable but somewhat unremarkable, noting in a letter to his wife Ruth that Irvine was reliable for "everything except conversation." However, this initial impression would change as the expedition progressed, with Mallory coming to appreciate Irvine's unwavering dedication, practicality, and strength.

The journey to Everest was grueling, requiring weeks of travel through the harsh Tibetan landscape. Irvine, like the rest of the team, endured long days of trekking across rugged terrain, battling altitude sickness and extreme weather. Along the way, he built rapport with the other team members and the local Sherpa porters, who appreciated his unassuming demeanor and work ethic. Lieutenant Colonel Edward Norton, the de facto leader of the expedition after Bruce fell ill, later wrote that Irvine's "cheerful camaraderie, his unselfishness and high courage made him loved, not only by all of us, but also by the porters, not a word of whose language could he speak."

As the team established camps along the North Col route, Irvine's practical skills and physical strength became increasingly vital. The heavy loads required for high-altitude climbs tested even the most seasoned climbers, but Irvine's remarkable fitness allowed him to carry significant burdens with relative ease. His role as Oxygen Officer also meant he was constantly inspecting and maintaining the apparatus, ensuring it would function reliably in the extreme conditions near the summit.

While Irvine's mechanical expertise made him indispensable, his limited climbing experience remained a concern for some members of the team. Nevertheless, his determination to prove himself overshadowed any doubts. Irvine approached each challenge with a blend of optimism and resolve, embodying the adventurous spirit celebrated in British exploration at the time. His willingness to embrace hardship and risk earned him the admiration of his peers and the trust of Mallory, who chose Irvine as his partner for the final summit push.

The decision to pair Mallory with Irvine for the summit attempt was both strategic and symbolic. Mallory, the seasoned mountaineer, brought years of experience and a deep understanding of the mountain, while Irvine's youth, strength, and technical expertise with the oxygen systems complemented Mallory's skills. Together, they represented the past and future of British mountaineering – a partnership that symbolized the country's enduring ambition and ingenuity.

The fateful summit attempt began in early June 1924. As Mallory and Irvine ascended from the higher camps, their progress was closely monitored by Noel Odell, who was stationed at Camp VI. On June 8, Odell reported seeing the pair ascending what he believed to be the Second Step, moving with apparent strength and determination. His sighting marked the last confirmed observation of Mallory and Irvine before they disappeared into the mists near the summit, leaving their ultimate fate shrouded in mystery.

Irvine's youth and relative inexperience made his inclusion in such a dangerous undertaking a point of contention among some historians. However, his presence on the expedition and his contributions to the team's efforts were undeniable. Irvine embodied the adventurous ethos of his time – a willingness to confront the unknown and push the limits of human endurance, even at great personal risk.

The tragedy of Mallory and Irvine's disappearance has only added to Irvine's legacy, casting him as a symbol of youthful courage and unfulfilled potential. Family friend Sir Arnold Lunn reflected on Irvine's short but impactful life, writing: "Irvine did not live long, but he lived well. Into his short life he crowded an overflowing measure of activity which found its climax in his last wonderful year, a year during which he rowed in the winning Oxford boat, explored Spitsbergen, fell in love with skiing, and – perhaps – conquered Everest. The English love rather to live well than to live long."

The possibility that Irvine and Mallory reached the summit before their untimely deaths continues to captivate mountaineers and historians alike. While definitive proof has yet to be discovered, Irvine's technical expertise and determination were pivotal to their final ascent. His reconfigured oxygen systems, although not officially adopted by Siebe Gorman, may have been used during the climb and could have provided a crucial advantage in the thin air near the summit.

Irvine's legacy as the "young engineer of Everest" endures, not only for his contributions to the 1924 expedition but also for the inspiration he provides to adventurers and innovators. Lieutenant Colonel Norton summed up the sentiment of those who knew Irvine best, writing: "Young Irvine was almost a boy in years – he was twenty-two, but mentally and physically he was a man full grown... His cheerful camaraderie, his unselfishness, and high courage made him loved."

Though his life was tragically cut short, Andrew Irvine's story is one of ambition, resilience, and the pursuit of greatness. His name remains etched in the annals of mountaineering history, a testament to the enduring allure of Everest and the indomitable spirit of those who dare to scale its heights.

Chart of Irvine's Climbing Experience Prior to Everest

Year of Climb	Activity Location Description	Significance/Skills Gained
1923 Napes Needle	Lake District, England Irvine climbed Napes Needle, a famous rock climb in the Lake District, under the supervision of experienced climbers.	This was Irvine's first notable climb. This climb introduced him to basic rock climbing techniques and the safety protocols that come with them.
1923 Snowdonia Wales	Took part in some climbs in Snowdonia, a mountainous region in Wales	These climbs provided Irvine with basic experience in mountain terrain, however were of little

| | | mountaineering or technical challenge. |

Responsibility Description Impact on the Expedition

Responsibility	Description	Impact on Expedition
Oxygen System Development & Maintenance	Irvine was responsible for modifying and improving the oxygen apparatus used during the climb. He enhanced the efficiency and durability of the oxygen systems, which were critical for survival at high altitudes.	Irvine's modifications allowed for a lighter, more reliable oxygen system, increasing the climbers' endurance and extending their high-altitude range.
Support Climber and Porter	As a support climber, Irvine helped ferry supplies to and from the higher camps (Camp IV and Camp V), assisting in setting up summit attempts for George Mallory and other lead climbers, prior to his own climb with Mallory.	His contributions allowed other climbers, particularly George Mallory, to focus on summit attempts without being burdened by carrying heavy equipment. This role also tested Irvine's high-altitude endurance.
Equipment Transport and Assembly	As one of the younger, stronger members, Irvine was tasked with carrying heavy loads of equipment, including oxygen cylinders, up the mountain. He was also involved in setting up the oxygen systems at various camps. He was referred to as an experiment by both Bruce and Mallory	His role here was crucial, as his logistical support enabled the higher camps to be fully equipped for the summit attempts.
Tinkering and Mechanical Adjustments	Irvine was responsible for troubleshooting and repairing mechanical equipment, including oxygen sets and other technical gear, which often malfunctioned in extreme conditions.	Irvine's engineering skills made him the expedition's "fixer" for any malfunctioning equipment, ensuring that no technical failures would impede the climbers' progress
Camp Setup and Maintenance	Irvine assisted in establishing and maintaining the higher-altitude camps (e.g., Camp IV and V), where climbers rested before final summit pushes.	By helping set up higher camps, Irvine played a key role in ensuring that the expedition had safe, functional resting points, which were crucial for acclimatization and logistics.
Recording and Documenting Equipment Use	Irvine took part in documenting the oxygen system's performance and its effectiveness in high-altitude conditions, an essential aspect of	These records would have contributed valuable data on oxygen usage and its effects on human physiology at high altitudes, but the full extent of Irvine's

		scientific research during the expedition.	documentation was lost after he and Mallory disappeared.
Summit Partner to George Mallory		Despite his limited mountaineering experience compared to others, Irvine was chosen as Mallory's summit partner for the final push toward the peak due to his physical strength and compatibility.	This decision highlighted Irvine's fitness and the trust Mallory placed in his abilities, underscoring his critical role in the expedition's most daring attempt. This also reflected Irvine's adaptability in extreme situations.

Tyler Long

Chapter Four: The 1921 and 1922 Expeditions – Learning from Failure

The 1921 and 1922 British expeditions to Mount Everest marked the beginning of humanity's direct confrontation with the world's highest peak. These two expeditions were not just a physical challenge but also an immense logistical, scientific, and psychological undertaking. The efforts laid the groundwork for future attempts to conquer Everest, including the legendary 1924 expedition, but they were also fraught with setbacks and tragedy that shaped the narrative of mountaineering history.

The 1921 reconnaissance expedition was an unprecedented endeavor, fueled by the Mount Everest Committee's success in raising £10,000, equivalent to approximately £600,000 today. This funding enabled the team to be equipped with the best gear available at the time, including specialized tents, clothing, boots, and ropes. The expedition departed England in April 1921, led by Charles Howard-Bury after Charles Granville Bruce, the original leader, was forced to remain in military service. While Charles Howard-Bury served as the official leader of the expedition, it was George Mallory – who thought expedition leader Charles Howard-Bury to be a snob and inflexible due to his cautious approach – who quickly emerged as the de facto lead climber due to his exceptional climbing abilities and leadership under high-altitude conditions despite his lack of experience in the Himalayas (Johnson, 2022).

Howard-Bury documented the expedition's achievements and insights in his book, *Mount Everest: The Reconnaissance, 1921*, to which Mallory contributed six chapters, showcasing both his observations and aspirations for Everest's eventual ascent (Parker, 2023). The team consisted of a mix of scientists, climbers, and surveyors, including Mallory and Guy Bullock, both newcomers to

Himalayan exploration, and seasoned mountaineers like Harold Raeburn and Alexander Kellas. The broader team also included naturalist Dr. Sandy Wollaston, geologist Alexander Heron, and surveyors Captain Henry Morshead and Major Oliver Wheeler.

Their journey to Everest involved a six-week, 200-mile trek from Darjeeling through the harsh Tibetan landscape to reach the Rongbuk region. At the time, Nepal was closed to foreign travelers, forcing the team to approach Everest from the north through Tibet (Davis, 2020). Alexander Kellas had been sick for about a week, initially thought to be suffering from an inflamed small intestine. Tragically, Kellas died of heart failure on June 5, 1921, near the village of Kampa Dzong, Tibet. His death was a great shock to the expedition team, as he was the most experienced climber among them and a leading authority on high-altitude physiology, with pioneering studies that advanced global understanding of altitude sickness.

It was Kellas who first recognized the superiority of Sherpas as climbers and guides, a contribution that profoundly shaped future Himalayan expeditions. Well-liked and respected by all members of the team, Kellas was buried on a stony hillside overlooking the Tibetan plains, with a view of three Himalayan peaks he had climbed.

Dysentery plagued the group, leading to Raeburn stepping down as climbing leader. Mallory, though inexperienced in Himalayan conditions, assumed leadership in his stead, a role he filled with remarkable capability.

The expedition had three main objectives: to chart viable access routes to Everest, assess possible paths for a future summit attempt, and, if conditions allowed, make the first ascent of the peak. However, much of the region was uncharted territory. The team's first task was to map the terrain, which was accomplished through extensive surveying by Morshead and Wheeler, who together charted over 31,000 square kilometers. The lack of existing maps meant that every step of the journey doubled as a pioneering effort in geography.

The climbers' exploration began with the Rongbuk Glacier, which proved to be a challenging maze of icefalls and crevasses. Early attempts to ascend via the central approach revealed a 10,000-foot vertical wall of snow and rock, forcing the team to abandon the route. Mallory and Bullock then turned their attention to the eastern approaches, navigating the Kama and Kharta Valleys. In the Kangshung Valley, Mallory was struck by the sight of Everest's sheer eastern face, describing it as a "prodigious white fang." However, the

Kangshung Face's towering cliffs and unstable ice fields made it an impractical route. The climbers eventually identified the East Rongbuk Glacier and the North Col as the most promising approach to the summit. This discovery, credited largely to Oliver Wheeler, provided critical insights into Everest's topography and potential climbing routes.

Despite the team's pioneering efforts, the 1921 expedition faced logistical challenges and harsh environmental conditions that ultimately limited their progress. Mallory, Bullock, and Wheeler made a final push to an altitude of 23,000 feet before retreating. The winds and freezing temperatures on the North Col were relentless, and their supplies were nearly exhausted (Gray, 2019). Mallory described the scene in a letter to his wife Ruth: "Blown snow endlessly swept over grey slopes, just the grim prospect, no respite, and no hope." The expedition ended without a summit attempt but succeeded in mapping 12,000 square miles of previously uncharted territory and confirming a viable route for future expeditions.

The 1922 expedition built on these findings, with a more focused goal of reaching the summit. Led by Brigadier-General Charles Bruce, the team included several veterans of the 1921 effort, including Mallory, Morshead, and Wheeler, along with new members like George Ingle Finch and Edward Norton. This expedition marked the first use of supplemental oxygen in high-altitude climbing (Smith 2021), a controversial innovation that divided the team. Finch, a chemist, advocated for its use, arguing that it could enhance performance and endurance. The oxygen systems, designed by Georges Dreyer, were heavy and prone to malfunction, but their use allowed Finch and his climbing partner, Geoffrey Bruce, to reach a record altitude of 27,316 feet.

Name	Function on the 1922 Expedition	Profession in Life
Charles G. Bruce	Head of Expedition	Soldier (officer, Brigadier-General)
Edward Lisle Strutt	Deputy head of Expedition, Mountaineer	Soldier (officer, Lieutenant-Colonel)
George Mallory	Mountaineer	Teacher
George Ingle Finch	Mountaineer	Chemist (Imperial College London)
Edward "Teddy" F. Norton	Mountaineer	Soldier (Officer, rank: Major)
Henry T. Morshead	Mountaineer	Soldier (Officer, rank: Major)
Dr Howard Somervell	Mountaineer	Medicine
Dr Arthur Wakefield	Mountaineer	Medicine
John B. L. Noel	Photographer, Movie Camera Operator	Soldier (Officer, Captain)
Geoffrey Bruce (cousin of Charles G. Bruce)	Translator and Organisational Tasks	Soldier (Officer, rank: Captain)
C. John Morris	Translator and Organisational Tasks	Soldier (Officer, rank: Captain)
Colin Grant Crawford	Translator and Organisational Tasks	Officer of the British Civil Colonial Government
Dr Tom G. Longstaff	Expedition Doctor	Medical Doctor

The expedition began its ascent in April 1922, taking advantage of the narrow pre-monsoon climbing window. Camps were established at increasingly higher altitudes, culminating in Camp IV at 24,480 feet. From here, the team launched three summit attempts. On the 19th of May, 1922, George Mallory, Howard Somervell, Edward Norton, and Henry Morshead set off on their summit attempt, relying solely on their physical endurance and climbing skill. They were supported by a group of nine porters, departing from Camp III at 8:45 a.m. under favorable weather conditions. By 1:00 p.m., the men had reached the North Col, where they established a temporary campsite. As they planned for the following day, the team opted to carry only essential supplies, including two small tents, double sleeping bags, provisions sufficient for 36 hours, a gas stove, and thermos bottles (Young, 2022; Lee, 2020).

The next morning, Mallory awoke at 5:30 a.m., eager to begin the climb, but the porters had suffered from poor ventilation in their tents, limiting oxygen flow, and only five felt capable of continuing. Additional delays due to food preparation postponed the departure until 7:00 a.m. As the group ascended, the weather worsened, and temperatures plummeted. The terrain above the North Col was uncharted, and the team struggled to cut steps into the ice. These challenges led them to abandon plans for a camp at 26,000 feet and instead set up Camp V at 25,000 feet. While Somervell and Morshead found a relatively flat spot, Mallory and Norton were forced to pitch their tent on a steep incline. After setting up Camp V, the porters, struggling with the cold, were sent back down the mountain (Roberts, 2021; Foster, 2022).

On May 21st, the team resumed their ascent, leaving their sleeping bags at 6:30 a.m. and preparing to climb by 8:00 a.m. However, during preparations, a rucksack containing food supplies slipped down the slope. Morshead, despite the cold, retrieved the bag, but the effort left him too exhausted to continue. Mallory, Somervell, and Norton pressed on alone, aiming to follow the North Ridge toward the Northeast Ridge. Conditions were poor, with light snowfall. By 2:00 p.m., they had reached a point 150 meters below the ridge but decided to turn back at 26,985 feet, setting a new world record for high-altitude climbing. By 4:00 p.m., they had returned to Camp V, but their descent was fraught with danger. Most of the climbers lost their footing and slid down the slope, but Mallory's quick thinking with his rope and ice axe prevented a tragedy. The team made it back to Camp V in the dark, navigating a perilous crevasse field just above the camp. On May 22, after reaching an altitude of 26,800 feet, the team began their descent at 6:00 a.m. from the North Col (Evans, 2019; Taylor, 2021).

Expedition To The Unknown: Mallory And Irvine

The second attempt, led by George Finch, Geoffrey Bruce, and Gurkha officer Tejbir Bura, utilized supplemental oxygen and achieved a new altitude record. After regaining his health, Finch selected Bruce and Tejbir, as no other skilled mountaineers were available. On May 20th, the trio arrived at Camp III to inspect and prepare the oxygen equipment. By May 24th, they reached the North Col, where they rested before beginning their summit bid the next morning. Setting out at 8:00 a.m. on May 25th, they climbed the North Ridge toward the Northeast Ridge, accompanied by twelve porters carrying oxygen cylinders and supplies. Despite high winds, the oxygen systems allowed Finch, Bruce, and Tejbir to ascend quickly, although the porters struggled under the conditions. That evening, worsening weather forced them to halt at 24,480 feet and establish a temporary camp.

On May 27th, with supplies dwindling, the team resumed their climb at 6:30 a.m. under bright but windy conditions. Tejbir, inadequately equipped for the cold, collapsed at 26,000 feet and was sent back to camp. Finch and Bruce pressed on unroped for maneuverability. Reaching 26,080 feet, Finch redirected their route to avoid the worst winds, guiding them onto the North Face toward what is now called the Norton Couloir. Despite significant horizontal progress, they failed to gain additional altitude. At 27,316 feet, Bruce's oxygen apparatus malfunctioned, and Finch, noticing his partner's exhaustion, decided to descend. They returned to the North Col by 4:00 p.m. and reached Camp III an hour and a half later, setting a new altitude record and demonstrating the transformative potential of supplemental oxygen (Smith, 2021; Roberts, 2020; Evans, 2019).

Finch and Bruce's success had a profound impact on mountaineering. While some expedition members initially dismissed the use of oxygen as dishonorable – one committee member remarked,

"Only rotters would use oxygen" – the results proved its value. Oxygen allowed even relatively inexperienced climbers to achieve record heights, paving the way for its continued use in 1924 and beyond (Brown, 2021).

The third and final summit attempt of the 1922 expedition ended in tragedy. On June 7, Mallory, Somervell, and Colin Crawford led a group of 14 Sherpas up the North Col following days of heavy snowfall. Despite concerns over the snowpack's stability and debate about whether it was safe to proceed, Mallory decided to push on. At 1:30 p.m., about two-thirds of the way up the headwall and 600 feet below the Col, a massive avalanche tore through the slope. Seven Sherpas were swept over an ice cliff to their deaths. Two others were miraculously pulled out alive, but the avalanche marked the first recorded fatalities on Everest. Mallory himself fell 150 feet but escaped injury. The tragedy cast a somber shadow over the expedition, serving as a stark reminder of the mountain's deadly unpredictability.

Mallory was devastated by the loss of the Sherpas. In letters[5] written after the incident, he reflected on the enormity of the disaster, grappling with his responsibility as a leader. The loss underscored the lethal risks of high-altitude climbing, particularly the unpredictability of avalanches. In his correspondence, Mallory admitted feeling profound guilt, describing the event as one of the darkest moments of his life. The deaths also drew criticism from the broader mountaineering community, with some questioning the ethics of exposing Sherpas to such extreme dangers for the sake of British ambition. The tragedy became a stark reminder of the human cost of exploration.

The psychological toll of the 1922 expedition extended beyond the immediate grief of losing team members. Many survivors experienced heightened anxiety about the mountain's dangers, yet they remained resolute in their desire to conquer Everest. Mallory, in particular, became more introspective following the expedition. His letters to Ruth reveal a mixture of determination and doubt as he reflected on the near successes and the profound challenges they faced. Despite the setbacks, he wrote passionately about the mountain's allure, calling it a "final problem" that demanded resolution. This internal conflict set the stage for Mallory's renewed commitment to Everest in 1924.

---

[5] Letter from George to Ruth Mallory, 9 June 1922

The 1922 expedition provided valuable lessons that informed future attempts on Everest. The use of supplemental oxygen, though controversial, emerged as a crucial tool for climbing at extreme altitudes. George Finch's record-breaking ascent demonstrated its practical benefits, even as skeptics argued it compromised the purity of mountaineering. Finch's modifications, including lighter tanks and improved flow control, laid the groundwork for further refinements in 1924, highlighting the role of innovation in overcoming Everest's physiological challenges.

Careful logistical planning also became a priority. The team's reliance on porters and Sherpas emphasized the necessity of a strong support network. However, the avalanche tragedy that claimed the lives of seven Sherpas led to a reevaluation of risk distribution among climbers and local workers. By 1924, the Mount Everest Committee implemented stricter safety protocols and fairer task assignments to reduce these risks. Unpredictable weather, marked by fierce winds and sudden storms on the North Col, forced the team to adopt strategies for rapid acclimatization and efficient movement between camps. These adaptations became essential for minimizing exposure to Everest's harsh environment.

Despite its setbacks, the 1922 expedition marked a turning point in Everest exploration. The establishment of high-altitude camps and the use of oxygen systems pushed the boundaries of mountaineering. The lessons learned from their struggles and tragedies shaped future attempts and reinforced Everest's reputation as the ultimate challenge for climbers.

Mallory exemplified the shift from cautious exploration in 1921 to determined risk-taking in 1922. His resolve deepened despite the dangers, believing Everest could be conquered. The deaths of the Sherpas, however, served as a grim reminder of the cost of such ambition, prompting ethical debates about the responsibilities of climbers and organizers. For Mallory and his team, the experience was both humbling and galvanizing, blending personal ambition with the collective pursuit of a shared goal.

As preparations began for the 1924 expedition, the lessons of 1921 and 1922 loomed large. The climbers were acutely aware of the challenges they faced, from the mountain's treacherous weather to the limitations of their equipment. Yet they remained undeterred, driven by a shared belief in the possibility of success. For Mallory and his team, Everest represented the ultimate test of courage, resilience, and ingenuity – a challenge that demanded everything they could give.

The 1921 and 1922 expeditions thus set the stage for the defining moments of 1924. They revealed the mountain's immense difficulties while also demonstrating the potential for human achievement in the face of adversity. Through their failures and triumphs, the climbers forged a path that would inspire generations of adventurers, transforming Everest into a symbol of human aspiration and endurance. For Mallory, the lessons of these early expeditions were indelibly etched into his mind, preparing him for the ultimate challenge that lay ahead.

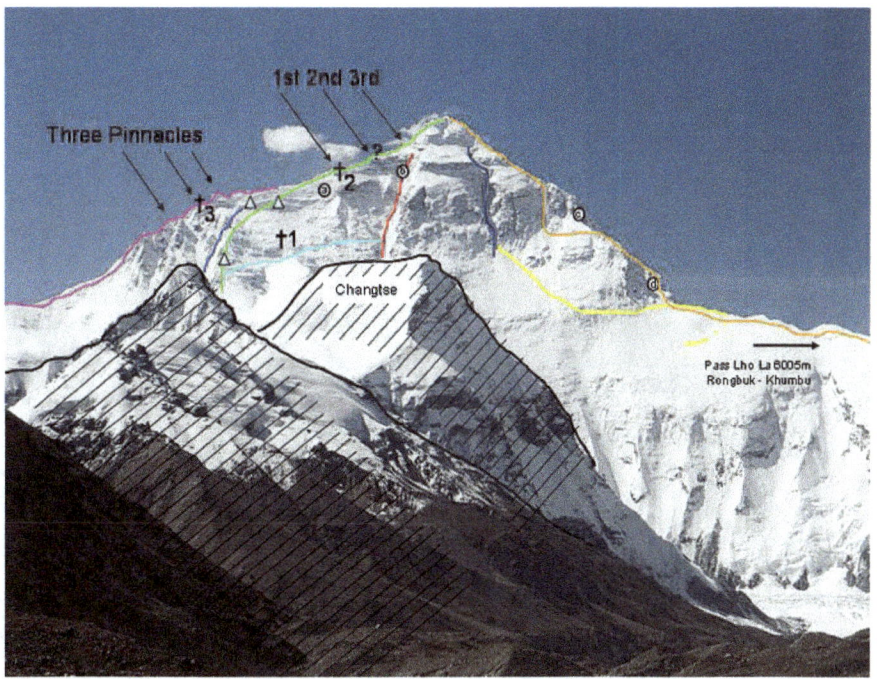

Tyler Long

Chapter Five:
The 1924 Expedition Begins – Assembling the Dream Team

The 1924 British Mount Everest expedition, often hailed as one of the most ambitious and tragic undertakings in mountaineering history, assembled a team that would go down in legend. This "Dream Team" comprised seasoned mountaineers, military men, scientists, and a young, untested climber whose name would become inseparably linked to the mountain's mystery. Their collective purpose was clear: to succeed where the expeditions of 1921 and 1922 had fallen short and to claim the summit of the world's highest peak for Britain. The expedition was led by Brigadier-General Charles Granville Bruce, a veteran climber and soldier with deep ties to the Himalayas. Bruce's leadership and rapport with the Sherpa community made him an ideal choice to helm the mission, though fate would soon alter his role (Macfarlane, 2003).

Name	Function on the 1924 Expedition	Profession in Life
Charles G. Bruce	Head of Expedition	Soldier (officer, Brigadier-General)
Edward F. Norton	Deputy head of Expedition, Mountaineer	Soldier (officer, Lieutenant-Colonel)
George Mallory	Mountaineer	Teacher
Bentley Beetham	Mountaineer	Teacher
Geoffrey Bruce	Mountaineer	Soldier (officer, Captain)
John de Vars Hazard	Mountaineer	Engineer
R.W.G. Hingston	Expedition Doctor	Medical Doctor and Soldier (officer, Major)
Andrew Irvine	Mountaineer	Engineering Student
John B. L. Noel	Photographer, movie camera operator	soldier (officer, Captain)
Noel E. Odell	Mountaineer	Geologist
Edward O. Shebbeare	Transport officer, Interpreter	Forester

| Dr. T. Howard Somervell | Mountaineer | Medical Doctor |

Charles G. Bruce

Charles Granville Bruce, born in 1866 into a distinguished British military family, lived a life defined by adventure, resilience, and leadership. From an early age, Bruce exhibited a fascination with the rugged outdoors, a passion likely fueled by the military traditions of his lineage. His upbringing emphasized discipline, physical endurance, and the exploration of uncharted frontiers. These qualities would later serve him well in his dual careers as a soldier and mountaineer.

Bruce attended the Royal Military Academy, Sandhurst, before being commissioned into the British Indian Army. He joined the 5th Gurkha Rifles, a regiment known for its valiant service in challenging terrains. Serving with the Gurkhas, Bruce developed a profound respect for the culture and capabilities of these Nepalese soldiers. His bond with the Gurkhas not only strengthened his leadership but also deepened his understanding of the Himalayan region, where he would make significant contributions to early mountaineering.

Throughout his military career, Bruce distinguished himself in various campaigns across the Indian subcontinent, earning accolades for his bravery and strategic acumen. However, it was his passion for climbing that set him apart. Bruce became one of the earliest Western climbers to explore the Himalayas, participating in expeditions that laid the groundwork for future ascents. His involvement with the Alpine Club, particularly in establishing its Himalayan Committee, positioned him as a pioneer in organizing large-scale mountain expeditions.

Bruce's mountaineering career faced a significant setback during World War I, where he sustained a debilitating injury. Doctors doubted his ability to climb again, but Bruce's determination proved them wrong. After the war, he returned to mountaineering with renewed vigor, leading the British Everest expeditions of 1922 and 1924. His familiarity with Himalayan terrain, gained through years of exploration and service, was invaluable.

As a leader, Bruce was known for his charisma and ability to inspire those around him. His rapport with the Sherpas, whom he treated with respect and fairness, was especially noteworthy. Unlike many of his contemporaries, Bruce recognized the critical role of the Sherpas in mountaineering, advocating for their acknowledgment and fair treatment. This perspective earned him the trust and loyalty of the local communities.

The 1922 Everest expedition, under Bruce's leadership, achieved significant milestones, including record altitudes and the first use of supplemental oxygen in climbing. However, it was also marked by tragedy, as an avalanche claimed the lives of seven Sherpas. This event profoundly affected Bruce, reinforcing the inherent dangers of high-altitude exploration.

In 1924, Bruce once again led the British Everest expedition. Unfortunately, his health deteriorated due to malaria contracted early in the trek. Reluctantly, he passed leadership to Edward Norton but remained a guiding presence, providing moral support and strategic advice.

Bruce's legacy extends beyond his mountaineering achievements. He played a pivotal role in fostering the development of Himalayan exploration, bridging cultural divides, and championing ethical practices in climbing. His life was a testament to resilience, leadership, and a relentless pursuit of the extraordinary.

Edward F. Norton

Edward Felix Norton, born in 1884 in San Isidro, Argentina, to British parents, led a life that seamlessly combined military discipline with the daring spirit of an adventurer. The son of a diplomat, Norton's early years in South America were marked by exposure to diverse landscapes and cultures, experiences that likely shaped his adaptability and curiosity.

Educated at Charterhouse School, one of Britain's prestigious public schools, Norton excelled both academically and athletically. His discipline and leadership potential earned him a place at the Royal Military Academy, Woolwich, where he trained as an artillery officer. Commissioned into the British Army, Norton's career quickly progressed, earning him assignments in India, where he gained firsthand experience navigating challenging terrains.

Norton's mountaineering journey began in the Alps, introduced by his grandfather, Alfred Wills, a prominent mountaineer and former president of the Alpine Club. Under Wills' mentorship, Norton developed technical climbing skills and an appreciation for the challenges of high-altitude exploration. His climbs in the Alps honed his precision and stamina, qualities that would later define his approach to Everest.

During World War I, Norton served with distinction in the British Army, earning the Distinguished Service Order (DSO) and Military Cross for his bravery and leadership. His ability to remain calm under pressure and make calculated decisions in critical moments solidified his reputation as an exemplary officer. These traits translated seamlessly into his role in mountaineering, where the stakes were equally high.

Norton first joined the Everest expeditions in 1922 as part of the climbing team. His methodical approach and natural leadership quickly made him a key figure in the group. During the expedition, Norton climbed to an altitude of approximately 26,800 feet without supplemental oxygen, a record at the time and a testament to his physical endurance. His observations and recommendations during the expedition were instrumental in planning future climbs.

In 1924, Norton returned to Everest as deputy leader under Charles Bruce. When Bruce fell ill, Norton assumed full leadership of the expedition. His calm demeanor and strategic thinking guided the team through some of the most challenging phases of the climb. Norton's focus on safety and calculated risks stood in contrast to Mallory's bold, often impulsive style, highlighting the diverse philosophies within the team.

One of Norton's most remarkable achievements during the 1924 expedition was his solo climb to 28,126 feet on the North Face, without supplemental oxygen. This feat set a new altitude record that stood for decades, underscoring his exceptional resilience and skill. Despite the physical toll, Norton remained committed to the team, leading efforts to support Mallory and Irvine's final summit attempt.

Norton's leadership extended beyond the mountain. Upon returning to Britain, he played a significant role in documenting the expedition's achievements and advocating for continued exploration. His reflections on the ethical and logistical challenges of mountaineering contributed to broader discussions within the Alpine Club and the mountaineering community.

Edward Norton's life embodied the intersection of military discipline and the pursuit of human limits. His contributions to the 1924 expedition and his record-setting climb remain milestones in the history of Everest, a testament to his character and capability.

Bentley Beetham

Bentley Beetham, born in 1886 in Darlington, County Durham, was a man of multifaceted talents whose contributions to the 1924 British Mount Everest expedition extended far beyond his climbing ability. Raised in a family that valued education and exploration, Beetham exhibited an early curiosity about the natural world, particularly its avian inhabitants. This interest would later lead to his groundbreaking work as an ornithologist and photographer.

Educated at Stockton Secondary School, Beetham excelled academically and demonstrated an artistic flair that complemented his scientific inclinations. He pursued his higher education at Armstrong College in Newcastle, where he specialized in natural sciences. It was during this time that Beetham developed a passion for ornithology, which would define much of his professional and personal life.

Beetham's career as a teacher began at Barnard Castle School in County Durham, where he taught natural history and geography. His innovative teaching methods and infectious enthusiasm for the subject made him a beloved figure among his students. However, it was his extracurricular pursuits that truly set him apart. An accomplished photographer, Beetham combined his love of birds and photography to document their behavior and habitats, pioneering techniques that would influence future generations of wildlife photographers. His work earned him recognition in scientific and artistic circles alike.

In addition to his academic and photographic endeavors, Beetham was an avid climber. His introduction to mountaineering came through the rugged peaks of the Lake District, where he honed his skills on challenging routes. Over time, he expanded his climbing repertoire to include the Alps, tackling formidable ascents that tested his technical ability and endurance. It was here that Beetham forged a lasting friendship with Howard Somervell, a fellow teacher and climber who would later recommend him for the Everest expedition.

Beetham's meticulous nature and eye for detail made him an invaluable member of the 1924 British Mount Everest expedition. As a photographer, he captured some of the most iconic images of the journey, documenting not only the grandeur of the Himalayan landscape but also the daily struggles and camaraderie of the team. His photographs, many of which were later published, provided an intimate glimpse into the expedition, preserving its legacy for future generations.

Beetham's climbing skills, though secondary to his role as a chronicler, were nonetheless significant. His steady temperament and careful approach to the challenges of high-altitude climbing earned the respect of his teammates. He shared a tent with Howard Somervell for much of the expedition, their shared history and mutual understanding fostering a sense of stability amidst the harsh conditions.

Beyond his technical contributions, Beetham's reflections on the expedition added a layer of humanity to its narrative. His writings, characterized by a blend of scientific observation and emotional depth, revealed the profound impact of Everest on those who dared to climb it. Beetham's ability to articulate these experiences helped bridge the gap between the climbers and the broader public, making the expedition's story accessible and inspiring.

Bentley Beetham's legacy extends beyond his role in the Everest expedition. His work as an ornithologist, photographer, and educator enriched the fields he touched, leaving an enduring impact. Through his lens and his words, Beetham brought the wonders and trials of the natural world to life, inspiring others to explore, learn, and appreciate the beauty around them.

Howard Somervell

Howard Somervell, born in 1890 in Kendal, England, was a man of profound intellect, faith, and endurance whose contributions to the 1924 British Mount Everest expedition epitomized the spirit of exploration. Raised in a devout Christian household, Somervell was instilled with values of compassion, humility, and service from an early age. His father, a successful businessman, encouraged his son's academic pursuits while fostering an appreciation for the outdoors.

Somervell attended Harrow School, where he excelled in academics and athletics. His natural aptitude for science led him to study medicine at Gonville and Caius College, Cambridge, followed by further training at London's University College Hospital. Specializing in surgery, Somervell demonstrated remarkable skill and precision, qualities that would later prove invaluable during his mountaineering exploits.

Beyond his medical career, Somervell was an accomplished climber. His introduction to mountaineering came through the Lake District and Snowdonia, where he tackled challenging routes that tested his physical and mental stamina. A member of the Alpine Club, Somervell expanded his climbing horizons to the Alps, honing techniques that would prepare him for the rigors of high-altitude expeditions. His calm demeanor and philosophical approach to climbing made him a trusted companion on the mountain.

Somervell's dual expertise as a surgeon and climber led to his selection for the 1922 British Mount Everest expedition. There, he not only demonstrated exceptional endurance, reaching record altitudes without supplemental oxygen, but also tended to the medical needs of his team and the Sherpas. His role as a healer extended beyond physical injuries; Somervell's compassion and faith provided emotional support during the expedition's most trying moments, including the tragic avalanche that claimed seven lives.

In 1924, Somervell returned to Everest, his commitment to the mission undiminished. Partnering with close friend Bentley Beetham, Somervell brought not only his climbing expertise but also his unwavering moral compass to the team. He viewed mountaineering as a spiritual journey, one that demanded humility and respect for the natural world. His reflections on the moral implications of high-altitude exploration, including the risks posed to Sherpas and porters, highlighted his deep sense of responsibility.

During the expedition, Somervell's medical skills were in constant demand. He treated cases of frostbite, altitude sickness, and exhaustion, often under extreme conditions. His presence was a source of reassurance for his teammates, who relied on his calm judgment and steady hands. Despite the physical toll of climbing, Somervell remained focused on the welfare of the group, embodying the selflessness that defined his character.

Somervell's high-altitude stamina and resilience were on full display as he accompanied Edward Norton on a record-breaking climb to 28,126 feet without oxygen. Though they were ultimately forced to retreat due to the harsh conditions, the achievement stood as a testament to Somervell's capability and determination. His experiences during the expedition deepened his philosophical reflections, which he later shared in lectures and writings that inspired a generation of climbers and adventurers.

After Everest, Somervell devoted his life to service, working as a missionary doctor in India. There, he combined his medical expertise with his commitment to education and social reform, making a lasting impact on the communities he served. His contributions to both medicine and mountaineering earned him widespread respect and admiration.

Howard Somervell's life was a testament to the power of faith, perseverance, and compassion. His role in the 1924 expedition, as both a climber and a healer, exemplified the highest ideals of exploration. Through his actions and words, Somervell left an enduring legacy, inspiring others to pursue their dreams with courage and integrity.

Noel E. Odell

Noel Ewart Odell, born on December 25, 1890, in St. Leonards-on-Sea, England, was a man whose life epitomized the fusion of scientific curiosity and mountaineering ambition. From a young age, Odell demonstrated an affinity for the natural world, a passion that would shape both his career as a geologist and his achievements as a climber.

Odell pursued his education at Brighton College and later at Imperial College London, where he specialized in geology. His academic rigor and fascination with Earth's processes led him to an early career exploring geological formations in remote regions. His research took him to areas as varied as Greenland and the Atlas Mountains of Morocco, honing the resilience and adaptability that would serve him well on Everest.

In addition to his scientific pursuits, Odell developed a passion for climbing. Introduced to mountaineering through the rugged peaks of Snowdonia in Wales, he quickly advanced to more challenging terrains in the Alps, where he tackled technical ascents that showcased his skill and determination. By the early 1920s, Odell had established himself as a competent and dependable climber, earning recognition within the Alpine Club.

Odell's expertise in geology and climbing made him an ideal candidate for the 1924 British Everest expedition. As the team's geologist, he was tasked with studying the mountain's geological formations and contributing to scientific knowledge about the region. His role as oxygen officer further underscored his versatility, as he managed the expedition's supplemental oxygen systems, which were still in their experimental stages.

Odell's relationship with Andrew "Sandy" Irvine added a unique dimension to the expedition's dynamic. The two men, despite their differences in age and experience, developed a close friendship, bonded by their shared sense of adventure and technical acumen. Odell admired Irvine's mechanical ingenuity, particularly his modifications to the oxygen equipment, which proved critical to the expedition's progress.

On June 8, 1924, Odell became the last person to see George Mallory and Sandy Irvine alive. Stationed below their route, Odell caught a fleeting glimpse of the pair ascending a rocky ridge near the Second Step. His account of this sighting – describing them as making "a great spur" for the summit – has fueled decades of speculation about whether Mallory and Irvine might have reached the top before their tragic disappearance. Odell's observation remains one of the most enduring mysteries in mountaineering history.

Odell's contributions extended beyond his scientific and logistical roles. His calm demeanor and philosophical reflections provided a steadying presence within the team. Even as the expedition faced setbacks and tragedies, Odell maintained a sense of purpose, documenting his observations with meticulous detail and offering insights that enriched the expedition's narrative.

After Everest, Odell continued his work as a geologist, embarking on expeditions to the Arctic and Himalayas and contributing to the understanding of Earth's geology. His experiences on Everest shaped his outlook on exploration, reinforcing his belief in the importance of scientific inquiry and human perseverance.

Noel Odell's legacy lies in his dual identity as a scientist and adventurer. His geological research and mountaineering achievements stand as a testament to his intellectual curiosity and physical endurance. His sighting of Mallory and Irvine, shrouded in both wonder and sorrow, remains a poignant symbol of Everest's allure and the sacrifices it demands.

Geoffrey Bruce

Geoffrey Henry Bruce, born on December 18, 1896, in Shimla, India, was a military officer whose remarkable adaptability and determination earned him a place in the storied 1924 British Everest expedition. A cousin of Brigadier-General Charles Granville Bruce, Geoffrey grew up in a family deeply connected to both the British military and the Indian subcontinent. His early life in the foothills of the Himalayas may have sparked the seeds of his later mountaineering endeavors.

Bruce was educated at Wellington College in England, where he demonstrated strong leadership and athletic prowess. Following his schooling, he attended the Royal Military Academy, Sandhurst, before being commissioned into the Indian Army. As a soldier, Bruce served with distinction during World War I, earning the Military Cross for his bravery in the field. His military career imbued him with discipline, resilience, and the ability to navigate challenging environments – qualities that would later prove invaluable on Everest.

Though he had limited climbing experience prior to joining the Everest expeditions, Bruce's physical strength and mental fortitude made him a compelling choice for the team. His connection to his cousin Charles Bruce, the leader of the 1922 expedition, undoubtedly played a role in his selection. Despite his novice status, Geoffrey quickly proved himself an asset, reaching record altitudes alongside George Finch during the 1922 expedition. Their use of supplemental oxygen marked a turning point in high-altitude climbing, demonstrating its potential to enhance human performance in extreme conditions.

Bruce's experiences in 1922 prepared him for the challenges of the 1924 expedition. Though still relatively inexperienced as a climber, he had gained valuable insights into the demands of Everest and the importance of teamwork. His willingness to undertake arduous tasks and his ability to adapt to the mountain's brutal conditions earned him the respect of his teammates.

On the 1924 expedition, Bruce played a critical role in supporting the establishment of high-altitude camps and ferrying supplies. His military training and logistical skills were instrumental in organizing the movement of equipment and ensuring that the team was adequately prepared for their summit attempts. Bruce's resilience in the face of physical and environmental challenges underscored his commitment to the mission.

While Geoffrey Bruce did not play a prominent role in the final summit push, his contributions to the expedition were no less significant. His ability to endure the punishing conditions of Everest and his steadfast support for his teammates exemplified the spirit of camaraderie that defined the mission.

After the 1924 expedition, Bruce returned to his military career, serving in various capacities in India and Britain. Though he never pursued mountaineering with the same intensity as some of his teammates, his experiences on Everest left an indelible mark on his life.

Geoffrey Bruce's legacy is one of perseverance and adaptability. As a relative newcomer to climbing, he rose to the challenges of Everest with determination and courage, contributing to the broader efforts of the British expeditions. His role in pushing the boundaries of high-altitude exploration remains a testament to the strength of the human spirit and the allure of the world's highest peak.

John B. L. Noel

John Baptist Lucius Noel, born in 1890 into a distinguished British military family, was a trailblazer in the field of expedition photography and filmmaking. Raised in a household that valued discipline and service, Noel's early exposure to global landscapes through his father's military postings ignited his passion for exploration. As a young man, Noel attended the Royal Military Academy, Woolwich, before being commissioned into the British Army.

During his early military career, Noel was stationed in India, a posting that brought him closer to the majestic peaks of the

Himalayas. His fascination with the region deepened during a daring solo journey in 1913 when he disguised himself as a Buddhist pilgrim to explore forbidden Tibetan territories. This audacious venture, a testament to Noel's adventurous spirit and determination, marked the beginning of his lifelong connection to the Himalayas.

World War I interrupted Noel's pursuits, but his military service honed skills that would later prove invaluable on Everest. Following the war, he turned his attention to photography and filmmaking, recognizing the potential of visual storytelling to capture and share the awe-inspiring beauty of remote landscapes. His innovative techniques and artistic eye set him apart, making him a natural choice for the 1924 British Mount Everest expedition.

As the expedition's official photographer and filmmaker, Noel's role was both technical and creative. Armed with custom-built cameras designed to withstand Everest's extreme conditions, he documented every aspect of the journey, from the camaraderie of the climbers to the grueling challenges they faced. Noel's ability to capture the essence of the expedition extended beyond the physical landscapes; his photographs and films conveyed the emotional and symbolic weight of the team's quest.

Noel's work was groundbreaking in many respects. He utilized long-range lenses to capture climbers from significant distances, creating some of the most iconic images of the expedition. His footage of the Himalayan landscape, interspersed with scenes of local Tibetan culture, provided audiences in Britain with an unprecedented glimpse into a world few had ever seen. These visual records not only preserved the expedition's legacy but also inspired public fascination with Everest and the spirit of exploration.

After the expedition, Noel's film *The Epic of Everest* became a cultural phenomenon, showcasing the grandeur and peril of the mountain to audiences worldwide. The film's poignant portrayal of Mallory and Irvine's disappearance struck a chord with viewers, immortalizing their story while highlighting the expedition's sacrifices and achievements.

Beyond his visual contributions, Noel played a crucial role in fostering connections between the expedition team and local Tibetan communities. His prior experience in the region and fluency in Tibetan facilitated smoother interactions, ensuring logistical challenges were met with cultural sensitivity and respect.

John Noel's legacy as a pioneering photographer and filmmaker endures. His ability to blend artistry with technical expertise and his dedication to preserving the human and natural story of Everest transformed the way such expeditions were documented. Through his lens, Noel captured not just the physical journey but the spirit of human aspiration, leaving an indelible mark on the history of exploration.

John de Vars Hazard

John de Vars Hazard, born on August 18, 1888, spent much of his early life in France before receiving his education at Bedford School in England and later studying engineering at Leeds University. From a young age, Hazard displayed a passion for mountaineering, participating in significant pioneering climbs in England's Lake District. Notably, he accomplished the first ascent of Abbey Buttress on Great Gable in collaboration with Fred Botterill during Easter in 1909. This formative experience highlighted his growing skill and enthusiasm for high-altitude challenges. Hazard's expertise was integral to the success of the 1924 British Mount Everest Expedition. He served as the team's quartermaster, ensuring the smooth transportation of supplies and equipment – a daunting task given the remoteness and scale of the expedition. Hazard's involvement in Himalayan exploration was further solidified by his earlier association with Alexander Kellas and his participation in the 1920 Kamet expedition. His logistical acumen and high-altitude experience proved indispensable for the Everest attempt.

During the First World War, Hazard served with distinction in the Royal Artillery, where his leadership and bravery were exemplified during the Battle of the Somme in 1916. Serving as second-in-command to Henry Morshead, Hazard earned the Military Cross for his service. Morshead, who would later gain renown as a key figure in the early British Mount Everest expeditions, participated in both the 1921 reconnaissance and the 1922 climbing expeditions to Everest. Morshead's high regard for Hazard's abilities and character led him to strongly advocate for Hazard's inclusion in the 1924 Mount Everest expedition. R.W.G. Hingston, the team's doctor, provided critical medical support, addressing the physical toll of high-altitude climbing on both the climbers and their Sherpa companions.

Hazard and Morshead maintained a close friendship, and the two shared aspirations of climbing Everest together during the early expeditions of 1921 and 1922. However, by 1924, when Hazard finally received his long-anticipated invitation to join the British Mount Everest expedition, Morshead was unable to participate. His commitments to the Indian Survey, combined with severe frostbite sustained during the 1922 expedition, rendered him unavailable and unfit to undertake further climbing at such altitudes.

Edward O. Shebbaere

Edward Oliver Shebbeare, born in 1884, was a forester by profession and a man of extraordinary adaptability and resilience. His life was characterized by a deep connection to nature, a commitment to service, and an ability to navigate the complexities of remote and challenging terrains. These qualities made him an indispensable member of the 1924 British Mount Everest expedition as its transport officer.

Shebbeare's early career was spent in the Indian Forestry Service, where he developed a profound understanding of Himalayan landscapes and local cultures. His work involved managing vast tracts of forested terrain, often requiring extended stays in remote regions under harsh conditions. This experience not only honed his logistical skills but also deepened his appreciation for the interconnectedness of natural ecosystems and human communities.

Fluent in several local languages, including Tibetan, Shebbeare's linguistic abilities set him apart from many of his contemporaries. His fluency allowed him to communicate effectively with the Sherpas and other local workers, building trust and ensuring the smooth execution of logistical operations. His knowledge of Tibetan customs and culture further enhanced his role, as he navigated the delicate task of securing support and cooperation from local communities.

As the expedition's transport officer, Shebbeare was responsible for managing the movement of supplies, equipment, and personnel across some of the most inhospitable terrain on Earth. This role required meticulous planning, adaptability, and an unyielding commitment to the team's progress. Shebbeare's expertise in organizing porters and caravans ensured that the climbers had the resources they needed at each stage of the ascent, despite the logistical challenges posed by Everest's unforgiving environment.

Shebbeare's role went beyond logistics; he was also a mediator and problem-solver. His ability to address disputes and foster camaraderie among the diverse group of climbers, Sherpas, and local workers contributed significantly to the expedition's cohesion. His understanding of the physical and emotional toll of high-altitude work allowed him to advocate for the well-being of the porters, ensuring they were treated with respect and fairness.

The 1924 expedition tested Shebbeare's abilities to their limits. Transporting oxygen cylinders, food, and other essentials to increasingly higher altitudes required precise coordination and unrelenting effort. Shebbeare's logistical acumen ensured that each camp was adequately supplied, despite the challenges of unpredictable weather, treacherous terrain, and the sheer scale of the mountain.

After the expedition, Shebbeare continued his work in forestry and remained involved in mountaineering circles. His contributions to the Everest expedition, though often overshadowed by the climbers' feats, were critical to its progress and legacy. His ability to balance practical logistics with cultural sensitivity set a standard for future expeditions, highlighting the importance of collaboration and respect in exploration.

Edward Shebbeare's life was a testament to the power of adaptability, knowledge, and respect for others. His role in the 1924 Everest expedition exemplified the behind-the-scenes heroism that underpins great achievements. Through his efforts, Shebbeare not only supported the climbers' ambitions but also strengthened the bonds between cultures and communities, leaving a legacy of collaboration and perseverance.

***

Together, these individuals formed a diverse and determined group, united by a shared goal and an unyielding spirit of adventure. Their journey to Everest was not just a test of physical endurance but a profound exploration of human ambition, resilience, and the limits of possibility.

The preparation for the 1924 Everest expedition was a massive undertaking, requiring meticulous planning, resourcefulness, and the cooperation of numerous individuals and organizations. The Mount Everest Committee, responsible for overseeing the venture, played a pivotal role in securing the necessary funding, which amounted to over £11,000 – a significant sum in the post-war economy. Financial support came from various sources, including private donors, corporate sponsors, and public subscriptions, reflecting the expedition's national significance. However, in 1924, the Committee was strapped for cash, exacerbated by the collapse of the Alliance Bank of Simla in 1923, which had served as the primary banker for many British military personnel and explorers. This bank failure triggered a financial crisis that threatened the expedition's viability, as it had managed the funds and logistical expenses for the previous two Everest expeditions. In addition to this blow, there were concerns about the expedition's chances, given the two failed attempts on Everest in the past and the controversial decision to leave behind George Finch, who had climbed the highest during the 1922 expedition and was a key pioneer in the use of oxygen at high altitudes (Reed, 2014).

The expedition's financing required a multi-faceted approach. The Royal Geographical Society (RGS) and the Alpine Club, both of which viewed the venture as an opportunity to reinforce British prestige in global exploration, appealed to a sense of national pride, framing the conquest of Everest as a British endeavor. Private patrons were also motivated by the opportunity to associate themselves with one of the final frontiers of exploration. Notably, Captain John Noel, a non-climbing member of the expedition, invested £8,000 in exchange for the rights to photograph and film the expedition. This investment relieved the Everest Committee from the need to pay roughly £2,000 for film and photography. Noel subsequently raised additional funds by forming a film company and planning to recoup his investment through film tours. Moreover, several British manufacturers donated equipment, such as Burberry, which provided specialized clothing including gabardine jackets and windproof layers, critical for the climbers to withstand the harsh climate and conditions on Everest (Hansen, 2013). Johnnie Walker and Bovril contributed food and drink, with Bovril, a concentrated beef extract, serving as a high-calorie, nutrient-dense source of energy. Siebe Gorman, a British company specializing in breathing apparatus, supplied the essential oxygen systems that would play a key role in the expedition's summit strategy. This combination of institutional backing, private investment, and commercial support enabled the expedition to gather the resources necessary for its ambitious attempt on Everest.

One of the greatest logistical challenges was the transportation of supplies. With Nepal closed to foreign travelers, the team's approach to Everest was routed through Tibet, necessitating a lengthy and arduous trek. This journey involved the movement of over 4,000 pounds of equipment, including food, climbing gear, tents, medical supplies, and oxygen systems. Edward Shebbeare, the transport officer, organized hundreds of porters and pack animals to carry the loads across the rugged Tibetan plateau. His expertise in managing this complex operation was crucial to the expedition's success.

The team's preparations also extended to securing diplomatic permissions. The expedition relied on the goodwill of Tibetan officials, including the 13th Dalai Lama, who granted access to the region. British officials in India, including political agents stationed in Sikkim, facilitated these negotiations, ensuring smooth passage for the team and their supplies. This diplomatic effort highlighted the expedition's broader geopolitical context, as Britain sought to maintain its influence in the region while fostering goodwill with Tibet.

On the ground, the climbers underwent rigorous physical and mental preparation. Many had trained in the Alps, Snowdonia, or the Lake District to build endurance and hone their technical climbing skills. George Mallory, for instance, spent weeks leading up to the expedition climbing in Wales to improve his strength and agility. Andrew Irvine, though less experienced as a climber, worked tirelessly to master the use of oxygen equipment, which he had also modified to improve its efficiency.

The team's camaraderie was both a strength and a challenge. While their shared goal created a strong bond, differences in personality and approach sometimes led to tensions. Mallory, deeply committed to the mission, often clashed with Norton over strategy, while Irvine's youth and inexperience occasionally drew skepticism from older team members. However, these conflicts were balanced by moments of solidarity, such as the mutual respect between Mallory and Irvine, whose partnership symbolized the merging of experience and innovation.

The expedition officially began in late February 1924, with the team departing from Tilbury Docks aboard the SS California. Their journey took them to India, where they spent several weeks acclimatizing and organizing supplies in Darjeeling before embarking on the long trek to Everest. The climb through the Tibetan landscape was both physically demanding and awe-inspiring. John Noel captured the majesty of the region through his lens, producing some of the earliest and most iconic images of the Himalayan environment.

As the team approached the Rongbuk Monastery, the spiritual gateway to Everest, they were met with a mixture of excitement and apprehension. The monastery, a place of deep religious significance for the local Sherpas, served as a reminder of the cultural and spiritual dimensions of their journey. The Sherpas, whose support was indispensable to the expedition, were greeted with gratitude and respect by the team. Brigadier-General Bruce, known for his rapport with the Sherpa community, ensured that their contributions were recognized and valued.

On May 15, 1924, the expedition members received blessings from the Lama at the Rongbuk Monastery. Along with the blessing, however, came a stern warning. The Lama spoke of disaster to come, prophesying that the mountain's demons would delight in forcing the climbers off Everest. To emphasize his warning, the monks created a gruesome illustration showing mountain gods disemboweling a Western man and casting him into hell. For Mallory, a man who was not superstitious, this moment must have been deeply unsettling (Firstbrook, p. 154). On his third expedition to Everest, with its atmosphere saturated with signs of doom, it would have been difficult to dismiss the weight of these omens.

The climbers established their base camp at the foot of the Rongbuk Glacier, marking the beginning of their ascent. From here, the team faced the monumental task of navigating the treacherous north face of Everest, a region riddled with shifting glaciers, sheer ice walls, and unpredictable weather. The logistics of establishing intermediate camps were daunting. Supplies, including oxygen cylinders, food, and tents, had to be ferried to higher altitudes by porters, Sherpas, and the climbers themselves. Each camp represented a small victory over the mountain but also underscored the immense physical and psychological toll of the climb.

By May 19, Norton, Mallory, Somervell, and Odell arrived at Camp III. At this altitude, approximately 21,000 feet, the effects of thin air began to show. Each breath contained fewer oxygen molecules, leaving the climbers increasingly fatigued. Their appetite waned, and many developed splitting headaches (Anker, "The Wildest Dream," 2010). Conrad Anker, reflecting on such conditions, later remarked that "the simplest task would've become monumental." Around this time, the climbers encountered their first taste of bad weather. Sandy Irvine, inexperienced but resilient, wrote in his journal: "Had a terrible night, wind, and snow. I don't know how the tents stood it. Very little sleep, and about 2 inches of snow over everything in the tent. Awful headache this morning." Irvine's words illustrated not only the harsh conditions but also his likely battle with altitude sickness (Irvine, 1924). Mallory, ever optimistic, pressed on, knowing that the summit was still calling him from 9,000 feet above.

On May 21, the climbers began fixing ropes on the icy slopes leading to the North Col. Progress was slow and arduous, but by May

22, they had successfully erected Camp IV at a height of 22,970 feet. The team faced another bout of deteriorating weather, which pinned them down. John de Vars Hazard, left at Camp IV with twelve porters and dwindling supplies, faced an increasingly dire situation. Hazard managed to descend with eight porters, but four who had become ill were rescued by Norton, Mallory, and Somervell in a daring act of teamwork. The entire expedition returned to Camp I, where a group of fifteen porters, later dubbed "tigers" for their strength and resilience, was chosen for the next summit attempts.

The first summit attempt began on June 1, 1924, with Mallory and Bruce setting out from Camp IV, accompanied by nine tiger porters. As they ascended from the shelter of the ice walls, they were exposed to harsh, icy winds sweeping across the North Face. Before they could establish Camp V at 25,200 feet, four of the porters abandoned their loads, forcing Mallory and Bruce to make up for the shortfall. Mallory worked quickly to erect platforms for the tents, while Bruce and one remaining porter retrieved the discarded loads. The next day, three additional porters refused to climb higher, leaving the pair unable to establish Camp VI at 26,800 feet. The attempt was abandoned, and the pair descended, encountering Norton and Somervell on their way up.

The second summit attempt, led by Norton and Somervell, began on June 4. Departing from Camp VI at 26,700 feet in the pre-dawn cold, their day began poorly as Norton discovered one of his thermos flasks of warm tea had spilled overnight. Norton and Somervell opted for a traverse across the North Face toward the Great Couloir, diverging from Mallory's preferred route along the Northeast Ridge. Norton later described the early conditions as "fine and nearly windless" but "bitterly cold." The ascent was grueling; Norton suspected the approach of malaria as he struggled against the cold and exhaustion. At approximately 28,126 feet – just 918 feet below the summit – Norton turned back, citing the treacherous terrain and lack of supplemental oxygen as insurmountable obstacles (Firstbrook, p. 157).

Somervell, meanwhile, faced his own battle. Frostbite ravaged his larynx, leaving him gasping for air during the descent. He used a tent pole to perform a form of the Heimlich maneuver on himself, expelling the frozen lining of his throat and narrowly saving his life (Somervell, "After Everest"). Norton, suffering from snow blindness, struggled to navigate. Together, they managed to return to Camp IV after nightfall, their ordeal a testament to the immense dangers of high-altitude climbing without oxygen.

The stage was set for the final summit push. Mallory and Irvine, chosen as the lead pair, prepared themselves for the climb of their lives. Mallory's experience and determination, coupled with Irvine's technical expertise, made them a formidable team. As they left Camp VI on June 8, 1924, their fellow climbers watched with a mix of hope and apprehension, aware that this attempt could either make history or end in tragedy.

Chapter Six:
Into the Death Zone – Mallory and Irvine's Summit Attempt

The decision to attempt the summit of Mount Everest in 1924 was born out of a culmination of ambition, personal resolve, and an almost palpable sense of destiny. For George Mallory, Everest symbolized not just a peak to be conquered but the ultimate challenge of human endurance. For Andrew "Sandy" Irvine, the summit attempt was the pinnacle of an extraordinary adventure. As the two climbers prepared for their final ascent, their lives, personalities, and unique circumstances converged, creating an enduring narrative of exploration, ambition, and mystery.

The summit attempt followed a series of events that reshaped the trajectory of the expedition. Norton and Somervell's June 4 attempt had been planned as the final push, with no reliance on supplemental oxygen. However, the attempt exposed the brutal limitations of high-altitude climbing without oxygen, prompting Mallory to reconsider. Determined to give the mountain another try, he selected Irvine as his climbing partner, citing Irvine's unparalleled skill with the expedition's oxygen apparatus. The decision, while logical, underscored a significant gamble – Mallory was placing his fate, and perhaps his legacy, in the hands of a relatively inexperienced mountaineer.

In his last letter to his wife, Ruth, Mallory wrote with a mix of conviction and uncertainty:

"Dear girl,

This has been a bad time altogether. Perhaps it's mere folly to go up again. But how can I be out of the hunt? Six days to the top from this camp. It's 50 to one, but we'll have a whack yet and do ourselves proud.

Great love to you ever,

Your loving George."

This sentiment encapsulated Mallory's determination to succeed despite overwhelming odds, even as he acknowledged the perilous nature of their attempt. At 37 years old, and only days away from his 38th birthday, Mallory was a husband, a father of three – John, Barridge, and Claire – and a teacher. His poetic spirit and philosophical devotion to climbing were matched by his physical prowess and single-minded focus on Everest, which he saw as his ultimate mission.

Sandy Irvine, in contrast, was only 22 years old, a vibrant and energetic product of post-World War I Britain's "bright young things." Though Irvine had not experienced the horrors of war, he was shaped by a society in recovery and renewal (Summers 2024). His charm, technical skill, and determination made him an invaluable member of the team, despite his inexperience as a climber. Known for his skill in repairing and optimizing the expedition's oxygen apparatus, Irvine embodied youthful enthusiasm and ingenuity. As Davis noted in *Into the Silence*, "Mallory chose Irvine for entirely logical reasons, prioritizing his expertise with oxygen systems over climbing experience." Irvine himself seemed eager, perhaps driven by a mix of youthful invincibility and the allure of contributing to something historic.

In the days leading up to the summit attempt, Irvine's health showed signs of strain. Diaries and letters revealed he suffered from a sore throat, difficulty breathing, and raw, sunburned skin due to prolonged exposure at the North Col. Yet, Irvine remained resolute. On June 5, in what would be his last letter home, he wrote: *"It will be a great triumph if my impromptu apparatus gets us to the top. It has been very trying for everyone with terribly strong reflection off the snow. I prepared two oxygen apparatus for our start tomorrow morning."*

Before setting out, Mallory meticulously outlined his plans. Initially, he envisioned a two-party summit attempt, with one team using oxygen and the other climbing without it. However, this ambitious strategy, which required extensive logistical support and large numbers of porters, was abandoned as the team's physical condition and resources dwindled. Instead, Mallory simplified the plan to focus on a single attempt.

On June 6, 1924, Mallory and Irvine departed Camp IV with a group of eight porters. Their breakfast that morning consisted of fried sardines, biscuits, chocolate, and tea, an attempt to provide sufficient energy for the grueling climb ahead. Moving steadily upward, they reached Camp V, located at approximately 25,262 feet. Mallory, ever optimistic, sent a message down with the porters: *"There is no wind here, and things look hopeful."*

Early on June 7, the duo pushed further toward Camp VI, situated at approximately 26,800 feet in the death zone, where human survival is measured in hours due to extreme oxygen deprivation and the onset of necrosis.

Mallory and Irvine's approach to this final leg of the climb was meticulous. They carried two additional six-pound sleeping bags from Camp IV to Camp VI. Mallory's notes revealed the importance of these extra sleeping bags, not only for warmth but also as a contingency plan. If one climber were forced to retreat due to adverse weather, injury, or mechanical failure of the oxygen apparatus, the sleeping bags would allow them to shelter safely while the other pressed on toward the summit. This preparation reflected Mallory's recognition of the mountain's dangers, likely influenced by the harrowing experience of Howard Somervell, who had nearly died on June 4 while waiting for Edward Norton in worsening weather.

The duo also accounted for oxygen usage with equal precision. Mallory and Irvine had brought a fifth oxygen cylinder as a backup, ensuring they could extend their summit attempt beyond the conventional turn-around time if necessary. Mallory's decision to use oxygen highlighted his willingness to embrace modern technology as a means to achieve the summit. Irvine, a technical genius with the apparatus, had modified the design to be lighter and more efficient. His expertise ensured the team's survival above 26,000 feet relied not just on physical endurance but on mechanical innovation (Unsworth, 2000).

During this phase of the ascent, fellow climber Noel Odell followed them partway, assisting with supplies before returning to a lower camp. On the ridge, Odell found a discarded oxygen bottle left by Irvine, evidence that the duo was conserving their limited oxygen for the summit push. Cameraman John Noel also captured footage of Mallory and Irvine as they climbed with their porters into the death zone, appearing as tiny figures against the towering expanse of the mountain. These haunting images, alongside Odell's discovery of the oxygen bottle, underscored the deliberate planning and immense physical effort required at such an altitude.

High in the death zone, with the summit less than 2,000 feet above them, Mallory and Irvine pitched their last camp. Here, they left further instructions for Odell and John Noel. Mallory's message to Odell reflected both his characteristic thoroughness and an understanding of the precarious nature of their situation:

"We're awfully sorry to have left things in such a mess – our Unna cooker rolled down the slope at the last moment. Be sure of getting back to IV tomorrow in time to evacuate before dark, as I hope to. In the tent I must have left a compass – for the Lord's sake rescue it: we are here without. To here on 90 atmospheres for the two days – so we'll probably go on two

cylinders – but it's a bloody load for climbing. Perfect weather for the job! Yours ever, George Mallory."

Mallory also sent a message to John Noel, offering a final point of reference for their movements:

"It won't be too early to start looking out for us either crossing the rock band under the pyramid or going up the skyline at 8.0 p.m."

These notes, practical and optimistic, highlighted the careful coordination Mallory intended to maintain, even at the expedition's most perilous stage. As night fell on June 7, Mallory and Irvine rested in the thin, frigid air of the death zone, steeling themselves for the ultimate challenge.

Their partnership, forged in the crucible of necessity, reflected both their individual strengths and the trust Mallory placed in Irvine's technical abilities. Mallory, the seasoned climber with years of experience and a poetic devotion to the mountains, relied on Irvine's practical expertise with the oxygen systems to improve their chances of success. Irvine, though battling physical ailments, remained resolute and determined, driven by the opportunity to make history alongside his mentor.

Above them loomed the Northeast Ridge and the Second Step, the most formidable barrier to the summit. With their oxygen supplies carefully rationed and their route meticulously planned, Mallory and Irvine stood on the precipice of immortality. The next steps they would take would define not only their legacy but the future of high-altitude mountaineering.

Mallory and Irvine's equipment reflected the limitations of the era. Their clothing, though state-of-the-art for the time, was

Expedition To The Unknown: Mallory And Irvine

dangerously inadequate by modern standards. Mallory wore Burberry jackets modeled after those used by Antarctic explorers, while Irvine's jacket featured additional pockets for tools and small items. Both men wore hobnail boots and woolen puttees, which offered some insulation but were insufficient for the extreme cold of Everest's upper reaches. They carried two oxygen cylinders each, along with a single backup cylinder for emergencies. Additionally, Mallory carried a Kodak camera, intending to document the summit if they reached it.

WAS THE SUMMIT OF EVEREST REACHED?
Mr. Odell's Story, which is Now Being Told from the Lecture Platform

THE LAST PHASE OF THE EXPEDITION—IRVINE AND MALLORY SCALING THE FINAL HEIGHTS TOWARDS "THE CITADEL," WHICH, INDEED, THEY MAY ACTUALLY HAVE REACHED

On the morning of June 8, 1924, Mallory and Irvine set out for the summit. The exact time of their departure remains uncertain, but estimates suggest it was between 3:00 a.m. and 5:30 a.m. Michael Tracy's analysis suggests they planned to begin as early as 3:00 a.m. to ensure they would be visible to John Noel by 8:00 a.m., as Mallory had instructed. However, some historians, including Graham Hoyland, believe the pair left as late as 5:30 a.m., already behind schedule. If this was the case, they faced significant risk of losing critical daylight hours – a factor that may have sealed their fate.

The moon had set at midnight, and the climbers awoke fatigued from a restless night compounded by exhaustion, lack of appetite, and dehydration. Irvine was in poor health, suffering from diarrhea, a sore throat, and breathing difficulties. His sunburned skin had been flayed raw by exposure to the harsh conditions at the North Col.

For Mallory, the climb held deeply personal stakes. His wife Ruth's letter expressed her faith in his ability: *"I will be thinking of you as you set off the summit. I know you can achieve your wildest dream."* This sentiment underscored the emotional burden Mallory carried. Some historians believe that his determination was fueled by a desire to reconcile the inner conflict between his obsession with climbing and his love for his family. By summiting Everest, Mallory could achieve his lifelong ambition and finally return to Ruth with a sense of closure.

Hoyland suggests that Mallory's contemporaries had surpassed him in worldly achievements, and this climb represented his last chance for greatness. Mallory himself had expressed his resolve in a letter to John Noel: *"We are going to sail to the top this time, God with us – or stamp to the top with our teeth in the wind."* Yet, his persistent cough and Irvine's weakened condition added to the immense challenges ahead.

As they ascended toward Camp VI, Mallory and Irvine carried two oxygen cylinders each, along with a fifth cylinder as a backup. The plan was to use the oxygen strategically, conserving it for the final push. They had a cooker to melt snow for water, but their bodies were wasting away from the combined effects of altitude and exposure. Mallory left instructions for Noel to watch for them at 8:00 a.m., but the absence of a compass, which he either lost or forgot, complicated navigation. Without it, the duo likely had to delay their departure until first light.

The challenges of the northeast ridge were formidable. Above 27,000 feet, climbers encountered the Three Steps – steep, rocky formations that required technical climbing skills even in favorable conditions. The Second Step, in particular, was a nearly vertical climb of approximately 90 feet, presenting a significant barrier. Mallory's earlier letters revealed his confidence in navigating these obstacles, but the absence of modern equipment and the primitive nature of their oxygen systems made the task Herculean.

The Second Step, a nearly vertical 130-foot climb, remains one of Everest's most challenging sections. Mallory and Irvine, following the Northeast Ridge route, would have faced this formidable obstacle as they neared the summit. Of the Three Steps on the ridge, the Second is the most prominent, rising approximately 130 feet at an altitude of 28,250 feet. Its upper crux, a 16-foot vertical headwall slab, consists of brittle rock, making it a daunting challenge for any climber, especially at extreme altitudes. In 1924, without fixed ropes or ladders, Mallory and Irvine would have relied on rudimentary techniques, sheer determination, and mutual ingenuity to surmount it.

Edward Norton, who had attempted the ridge earlier in 1924, concluded that the Second Step, or the "Great Rock Step," was impassable. Many of Mallory's contemporaries shared this skepticism, questioning whether he could overcome the climb, especially with Irvine in tow. Today, however, many historians and mountaineers argue that the obstacle was not insurmountable for Mallory. Experts like Conrad Anker, who successfully free-climbed the Second Step in 1999, contend that Mallory's exceptional rock-climbing skills and experience made the ascent plausible. Jake Norton elaborates: *"In Mallory's day, using the tried-and-true ten fingers – or head-standing as the Chinese did in 1960 – was not only acceptable technique but used quite often. Combine those techniques with Mallory's obsession with reaching the top in 1924, and you have a strong case for them pulling it off."*

One compelling theory is that Mallory and Irvine might have employed a "courte-échelle" or shoulder-stand technique to surmount the Step, as later demonstrated by Chinese climbers in 1960. Advocates of this theory, including climber Andy Politz, argue that such a maneuver, combined with Mallory's expertise, could have enabled them to overcome the obstacle. Politz remarked: *"Could George Mallory have stood on Andrew Irvine's shoulders and reached the hand jam of hand jams? You couldn't have fallen out, even if both your legs popped off. That hand jam is so good, it's so natural. I don't think there's any trouble with them having climbed the Second Step with a shoulder stand."*

The argument gains further credence from Noel Odell's sighting of two climbers near one of the Steps on June 8, 1924. Odell later described the moment in vivid detail:

"At 12.50...there was a sudden clearing of the atmosphere, and the entire summit, ridge, and final peak of Everest were unveiled. My eyes became fixed on a small snow crest beneath a rock step in the ridge, and the black spot moved. Another black spot became apparent, and moved up the snow

to join the other on the crest. The first then approached the great rock step, and shortly emerged at the top; the second did likewise. Then the whole fascinating vision vanished, enveloped in cloud once more."

Odell's account of observing one figure moving "with alacrity" suggests that Mallory, at least, possessed the strength and technique to scale difficult terrain quickly, even at such extreme altitudes. This sighting supports the possibility that Mallory and Irvine could have navigated the Second Step, though it remains uncertain whether they achieved this with or without additional techniques.

Above the Second Step lay the summit snowfield, a featureless expanse requiring endurance and precise navigation to traverse. If Mallory and Irvine reached this point, they would have faced a final push of approximately 300 feet to the summit. Although technically less challenging, this stage of the climb demanded an extraordinary effort from climbers already on the brink of exhaustion. The combination of their skill, determination, and modified oxygen systems may have given them a chance, but the lack of confirmed evidence – such as a photograph or other marker – leaves the question of their success unanswered.

The mystery surrounding Mallory and Irvine's final hours has captivated climbers and historians alike for nearly a century. Their disappearance near the summit of Mount Everest marked not only the end of the 1924 expedition but also the beginning of an enduring enigma: Did they reach the top of the world before their tragic demise? While their fate remains unknown, the aftermath of their journey offers crucial insights into the hazards of high-altitude climbing and the enduring human spirit that drives individuals to conquer the unconquerable.

> Camp I.
> May 27 1924
>
> My dearest Ruth, this is going to be the scrappiest letter — a time limit for the mail has suddenly been put on. This morning when I might have been writing to you I was busy doing a communiqué at Norton's request, I find it an impossible task to write that sort of thing up here. Anyway such as it is you will have read it, so that is some satisfaction.
>
> Dear Girl this has been a bad time altogether — I look back on tremendous efforts & exhaustion & dismal looking out of a tent door onto a world of snow & vanishing hopes — & yet & yet & yet there have been a good many things to set on the other side. The party has played up wonderfully. The first visit to the North Col was a triumph for the old gang. Norton & I did the job — the cutting of course was all my part — so far as one can enjoy climbing above Camp III I enjoyed the conquest of the ice wall & crack the crux of the route, & making the steps too in the steep final 200 ft. Odell did very useful work leading the way on from the camp to the Col; I was practically bust to the world & couldn't have lead that half hour though I still had enough mind to direct him. We made a very bad business of the descent. It suddenly occurred to
>
> P.S. The parts where I break if important are put in to please you & not principally for that use.

One of the enduring aspects of this mystery is the weather's role during their final climb. The initial clear conditions observed by Odell were replaced by heavy clouds and snow later in the day, suggesting the possibility of a sudden storm. Historical meteorological records corroborate that weather conditions on Everest during early June can shift dramatically, often without warning. If a blizzard enveloped Mallory and Irvine near the summit, they would have faced plummeting temperatures and zero visibility, compounding the already perilous nature of their ascent.

The thin air of the death zone also exacerbated their physical vulnerability. Without adequate supplemental oxygen, climbers can quickly succumb to hypoxia, leading to confusion, impaired judgment, and physical exhaustion. Even with Irvine's modifications, the oxygen systems they carried were rudimentary by modern standards. If the systems malfunctioned or ran out of oxygen near the summit, their survival odds would have drastically diminished.

The unanswered question of whether Mallory and Irvine reached the summit has kept their story alive in popular imagination. For some, the possibility that they were the first to conquer Everest adds a layer of triumph to their tragic tale. For others, the lack of definitive evidence underscores the inherent risks and unpredictability of high-altitude climbing.

In the decades since 1924, numerous expeditions have sought to uncover more clues about Mallory and Irvine's fate. Despite these efforts, the mountain has guarded its secrets well. The allure of solving the mystery continues to draw climbers and historians to Everest, reflecting the enduring fascination with this extraordinary chapter in the history of exploration.

Mallory and Irvine's ascent represents not just a physical journey but a profound exploration of human spirit and ambition. Their courage and determination to push the boundaries of possibility, despite the overwhelming odds, have immortalized them as pioneers of high-altitude mountaineering. The enduring mystery of their climb serves as a testament to the indomitable drive to explore, achieve, and understand the world's most formidable challenges.

Expedition To The Unknown: Mallory And Irvine

Chapter Seven:
Disappearance and Death – Theories and Speculation

In The Epic of Mount Everest, Younghusband put it well:

"Mallory knew the dangers before him and was prepared to meet them. But he was a man of wisdom and imagination as well as daring. He could see all that success meant. Everest was the embodiment of the physical forces of the world. Against it he had to pit the spirit of man, He could see the joy in the faces of his comrades if he succeeded. He could imagine the thrill his success would cause among all fellow mountaineers, the credit it would bring to England, the interest all over the world, the name it would bring him, the enduring satisfaction to himself that he had made his life worth while. All this must have been in his mind. He had known the sheer exhilaration of the struggle in his minor climbs among the Alps. And now on mighty Everest exhilaration would be turned into exaltation - not at the time, perhaps, but later on assuredly. Perhaps he never exactly formulated it, yet in his mind must have been present the idea of "all or nothing." Of the two alternatives, to turn back a third

time, or to die, the latter was for Mallory probably the easier. The agony of the first would be more than he as a man, as a mountaineer, and as an arust, could endure."

– Sir Francis Younghusband, The Epic of Mount Everest

The disappearance of George Mallory and Andrew "Sandy" Irvine during their 1924 Everest summit attempt remains one of the most enduring mysteries in mountaineering history. As the two climbers ascended into the thin, unforgiving air of the death zone, they carried not only the hopes of their nation but also an immense personal drive to conquer the world's highest peak. Their journey – punctuated by moments of determination, ingenuity, and profound risk – ended in ambiguity, leaving behind tantalizing clues and countless questions.

Irvine stated himself before the expedition "If we can get within a couple hundred yards, if we can get that near, and if we can see the highest point clearly, we shall go for it. And if it is one-way traffic, so be it." Mallory may have had a premonition of his own death. He confided in everyone but his wife Ruth that he believed the 1924 expedition would be "more like war than adventure and I do not expect to return alive."

Speculation about the fate of George Mallory and Andrew "Sandy" Irvine began almost immediately after their disappearance on June 8, 1924, as they ventured into Everest's death zone. The final sighting of the pair, made by fellow climber Noel Odell, described them ascending near the Second Step on the Northeast Ridge, moving "with alacrity." This fleeting observation placed them tantalizingly close to the summit, just 800 feet below the top. Odell's description fueled hopes that they may have achieved their goal before tragedy struck. However, when they failed to return to the lower camps and their bodies were not found during the initial search, the expedition concluded with a grim acknowledgment of their loss. From that point onward, a variety of theories about what transpired began to emerge.

One prominent theory suggests the duo successfully summited but encountered disaster during their descent. Experts believe they may have reached the summit close to sunset after an arduous ascent. Exhausted from the climb and with monsoon clouds gathering, Mallory and Irvine began descending the summit pyramid in fading light. Their route took them past the Third Step, but the descent of the Second Step presented a formidable obstacle without modern fixed lines. This section, often cited as one of the greatest dangers of their journey, may have led to their downfall. It is theorized that Mallory lowered Irvine down the Second Step using their rope. As Mallory followed, Irvine may have provided a hip belay, but an accident could have occurred during this precarious descent. One possibility is that Mallory slipped, falling hard onto the snow platform below, sustaining injuries that would slow their progress further. Despite their injuries and the rapidly fading daylight, the pair pushed on, traversing ledges and descending the First Step in the dark, guided only by moonlight. Navigational errors in the darkness may have compounded their difficulties. Modern research suggests they likely selected the wrong set of gullies to descend from the ridge, which led them into steep cliff bands. Some theorists believe that Mallory attempted to lower Irvine with a rope again, but the rope broke, and Mallory fell to his death. Injured and likely hypothermic, Irvine may have sought shelter in a dihedral to wait for daylight, only to succumb to the extreme cold overnight.

Another hypothesis, proposed by Tom Holzel, suggests that Mallory, realizing Irvine's inexperience, made a calculated decision to send him back down the mountain while Mallory pushed toward the summit, utilizing both climbers' oxygen supplies. Holzel posits that Irvine could have been caught in a snow squall during his descent and fallen to his death, while Mallory, unaware of Irvine's fate, succeeded in summiting. However, Mallory's subsequent descent would have been fraught with peril, and the exact cause of his death remains uncertain in this scenario.

Wade Davis presents a more conservative view, doubting that Mallory and Irvine reached the summit. He points to evidence such as the discovery of an oxygen bottle below the First Step and the severe sunburn and exhaustion Irvine was reported to have endured. Davis argues that Mallory would never have abandoned Irvine, suggesting they likely turned back before reaching the summit. In this version of events, the pair may have encountered fatal missteps while descending from the Second Step.

John Noel states, "He's already, according to the plan they made, four hours late for the last ascent. He was going forward to the top, not returning back to the last camp on Everest. No human being can survive without his tent and sleeping bag at that altitude. They were at camp 27,000 feet above the sea. They had to get back to the camp that night. They never did."

Michael Tracy's theory, presented in his video, *Mallory & Irvine: The Watch*, provides a compelling narrative for the final hours of George Mallory and Andrew Irvine on Mount Everest, aligning with observations, physical evidence, and historical context.[6] He proposes that the duo's route, timing, and critical decisions contributed to their disappearance, offering a plausible explanation for what may have happened on June 8, 1924.

Tracy asserts that Mallory and Irvine opted for the zigzag route, first described by Edward Norton and later detailed by Howard Somervell in his 1936 book, *After Everest: The Experiences of a*

---

[6] https://www.youtube.com/watch?v=NIh6vP7fXMo

Mountaineer and Medical Missionary. The zigzag route provided a shielded ascent through the couloir, mitigating exposure to the brutal afternoon winds known to pick up on Everest's North Face. This deviation would have been a logical adjustment as they realized they were behind schedule and needed to adapt to the mountain's changing conditions.

The timeline begins with their delayed departure from Camp VI. Tracy argues that Mallory and Irvine did not leave by moonlight because the moon would not rise until after daylight. Furthermore, Mallory's compass, essential for navigation in pre-dawn darkness, had been left at a lower camp. Without the compass or sufficient moonlight, finding the crack in the Yellow Band – an essential navigational marker – would have been nearly impossible before sunrise. Tracy deduces that Mallory and Irvine departed Camp VI at approximately 5:30 a.m., aligning their start with the first light of day, which occurred at 5:13 a.m.

By 12:50 p.m., Noel Odell reported seeing two figures near the Third Step, moving "with alacrity." Tracy interprets this sighting as evidence that they had reached 28,450 feet after seven hours of climbing at an estimated rate of 250 vertical feet per hour. However, this placed them behind schedule, making it unlikely they could reach the summit before late afternoon. The delay, coupled with Mallory's intimate knowledge of Everest's weather patterns, likely spurred their decision to switch to the zigzag route, which would offer some protection from the anticipated afternoon winds.

Tracy's timeline reconstructs their climb beyond Odell's sighting. He theorizes that the pair reached the summit at approximately 5:30 p.m., just as the sun began to set. This late arrival would have placed them in a precarious position, as they now faced a descent in darkness, compounded by exhaustion and the cold of night. Sunset occurred at 7:08 p.m., and the moon set at 11:24 p.m., leaving them with limited visibility for the most treacherous sections of their descent.

One key piece of evidence supporting Tracy's timeline is Mallory's stopped watch, discovered in 1999 near his remains. The watch was frozen at 1:27 a.m., which Tracy believes marks the time of their fatal fall. Working backward from this moment, he concludes that Mallory and Irvine were forced to navigate the descent largely in darkness, slowing their progress significantly. The descent from the summit to the site of Irvine's ice axe – a location discovered in 1933 – would have taken 7–9 hours, meaning that by 2:30 a.m., they likely would have succumbed to their circumstances even if they had not fallen.

Tracy provides several reasons for believing the pair summited before their deaths. First, they had access to supplemental oxygen, a critical advantage at extreme altitudes. Tracy highlights Irvine's mechanical expertise with the oxygen apparatus as one of the main reasons he was selected as Mallory's climbing partner. This expertise would have allowed them to troubleshoot any issues with the equipment, giving them the best chance of success.

Second, the absence of Ruth Mallory's photograph – a detail George Mallory had promised to leave on the summit – is a poignant clue. When Mallory's body was found, letters to his siblings and other personal effects were recovered, but Ruth's photograph was missing. Tracy interprets this as strong evidence that Mallory fulfilled his promise by leaving the photograph at the summit.

Third, Tracy points to Odell's sighting as further confirmation that the pair were advancing toward the summit. Odell's observation of their progress near the Third Step suggests they were well on their way to achieving their goal. The fact that Mallory was found with his snow goggles in his pocket also supports Tracy's timeline, as it indicates he was descending in darkness, likely well after sunset.

Finally, Tracy draws on other circumstantial evidence, including Mallory's intimate knowledge of the mountain's weather patterns and the strategic adjustments they made to their route. The zigzag route's protection from the afternoon winds demonstrates their awareness of the challenges they faced and their willingness to adapt.

Tracy's analysis paints a picture of two climbers who, despite being behind schedule, pushed forward with determination and ingenuity. Their ability to navigate the summit pyramid, Third Step, and other obstacles before sunset suggests they were operating at the limits of human endurance. However, the combination of darkness, cold, and exhaustion ultimately proved insurmountable.

Mallory's stopped watch at 1:27 a.m. serves as a haunting reminder of the risks they faced. For Tracy, this time not only marks the moment of their fall but also symbolizes the end of an era in mountaineering – a time when ambition and courage were often the only tools available to conquer the unknown.

Jake Norton's account, steeped in his mountaineering expertise, paints a vivid picture of Mallory and Irvine's potential descent. He imagines them summiting at sunset, then carefully retracing their ascent route through the summit pyramid and past the Third Step. Norton theorizes that Mallory, the more skilled climber, lowered Irvine down the Second Step but slipped during his own descent, falling hard onto the snow platform. Injured but alive, the pair struggled on, navigating exposed ledges in the dark until they descended into the wrong gully system. Norton postulates that the final accident occurred when Mallory attempted to lower Irvine down another cliff band. In the process, the rope likely severed, and Mallory plummeted to his death. Irvine, left alone and injured, sought shelter but succumbed to the freezing conditions before dawn. Norton's theory aligns with evidence of injuries on Mallory's body and the positioning of his remains, as well as Irvine's ice axe being found along a likely descent route.

Sir Martin Conway, a highly respected mountaineer, evaluated the expedition's evidence shortly after Mallory and Irvine's disappearance. He concluded that the duo likely reached the summit, bolstered by Noel Odell's compelling eyewitness account of the climbers ascending near the Second Step and moving "strongly for the top." Conway's assessment reflected a prevailing hope among contemporaries that Mallory and Irvine had achieved their goal, even without material evidence to confirm it.

Sir Jack Longland added a significant perspective to this debate in 1933, following the discovery of Irvine's ice axe on the North Face at an altitude of approximately 27,760 feet. Longland speculated that the axe marked the site of a fatal accident, suggesting a key moment in their descent where the pair likely encountered insurmountable difficulties. The ice axe's placement along a plausible descent route supported theories that Mallory and Irvine were returning from the summit when tragedy struck.

Ann Bridge, also known as Cottie Sanders, was a contemporary and close friend of Mallory. She offers another perspective in her unpublished memoir. She argues that Mallory and Irvine must have summited, given Odell's sighting of them moving strongly near the summit ridge. Bridge finds it inconceivable that Mallory, who had already mounted the final obstacle, would not have completed the climb. She also highlights the discovery of Irvine's ice axe as evidence of their descent. However, as with other theories, the absence of definitive proof leaves her account speculative.

The most intriguing clue to whether Mallory and Irvine reached the summit is the absence of Ruth Mallory's photograph, which

George had promised to leave at the top as a personal and symbolic gesture. When Mallory's body was discovered in 1999 by an expedition led by Eric Simonson, the photograph was not found among his personal belongings, though other items, including letters, a pocketknife, and altimeter, remained intact. This absence has led to speculation that Mallory fulfilled his promise, leaving the photograph at the summit, though others suggest it could have been lost during his fall.

The discovery of Irvine's Kodak camera is another tantalizing possibility. Advances in forensic technology have raised hopes that any film within the camera could still be developed, providing a definitive record of their climb. However, despite decades of searching, Irvine's body and the camera remain elusive, buried somewhere in the unforgiving terrain of Everest's North Face.

Theories about Mallory and Irvine's fate also consider the severe environmental challenges they faced during their final ascent. The death zone, above 26,000 feet, is an inhospitable environment where human survival becomes profoundly compromised. Oxygen levels at this altitude are a mere third of those at sea level, leading to hypoxia, which impairs cognition, respiration, and physical coordination. In such conditions, climbers are forced to make life-and-death decisions with significantly reduced mental and physical faculties. Temperatures plunge to -30°C (-22°F), and with winds gusting up to 100 mph, the chill is exacerbated, adding to the climbers' suffering. The intense cold, combined with the harsh winds, increases the likelihood of frostbite, hypothermia, and ultimately death. As Mallory and Irvine ascended, they faced these challenges in the most extreme of conditions.

Julie Summers, Irvine's great-niece and an author on the subject, argues that these environmental factors, combined with situational and personal challenges, make it extremely unlikely that Mallory and Irvine reached the summit. She points to several key obstacles, beginning with the low barometric pressure recorded on the mountain that day, which would have made breathing and physical exertion even more difficult. She highlights the Second Step as a formidable obstacle, one that has challenged even experienced modern climbers with the aid of fixed ropes and ladders. Adding to this was Irvine's relative inexperience. While he was reportedly as "strong as a horse," Summers emphasizes that physical strength alone would not have been sufficient for the technical and strategic demands of the climb.

On June 8, 1924, the weather, initially favorable, began to deteriorate in the afternoon, with clouds enveloping the summit, reducing visibility and complicating navigation. Some theories suggest that Mallory and Irvine were caught in a sudden and severe storm, which would have drastically diminished their ability to survive and navigate. Graham Hoyland and GW Kent Moore have studied how weather conditions impacted the duo's climb. Hoyland contends that a dramatic drop in barometric pressure around 2:00 PM, possibly due to a blizzard, played a significant role in their downfall. Barometric pressure readings taken at Base Camp during the expedition showed disturbances in atmospheric pressure, suggesting the presence of a storm that may have intensified as the climbers approached the summit. Hoyland's research underscores the critical balance required for survival in the death zone, where even small fluctuations in atmospheric pressure can exacerbate hypoxia, making the already grueling conditions even more perilous (Hoyland).

In fact, the 1924 expedition was among the first to collect meteorological data in the Everest region, with Howard Somervell recording crucial data that was later published in 1926. It wasn't until Kent Moore's 2010 study that the atmospheric pressure data was analyzed in the context of Mallory and Irvine's disappearance. This study revealed an 18 mbar drop in pressure recorded at Base Camp, likely signaling a far more dangerous storm at higher altitudes. Hoyland calculated that the minimum summit pressure during the storm would have been around 331 mbar, and as Dr. John Semple notes, a mere 4 mbar drop can lead to severe hypoxia, further impeding the climbers' ability to make rational decisions or continue their ascent (Hoyland; Moore, 2010).

The conditions were made even more brutal by unseasonably severe weather during May 1924. Reports from Darjeeling tea planters described weather patterns that were unprecedented in over two decades. Mallory and Irvine had already been forced to retreat from Camp III below the North Col due to intense storms that struck between May 9th and 11th. Persistent snowfall and a delayed monsoon created an environment that allowed for a summit attempt, but only in worsening conditions. According to Hoyland, these storms likely hampered the climbers' chances of survival on their return journey. The drop in pressure that coincided with their ascent on June 8th created additional challenges, with both climbers' physiological states further compromised as the storm intensified. Hoyland contends that Mallory and Irvine were caught in this blizzard, with diminishing visibility, extreme exhaustion, and hypothermia further reducing their ability to function effectively (Hoyland; Moore, 2010).

Given the conditions – severe hypoxia, exhaustion, exposure to the cold, and the relentless storm – survival at these altitudes was nearly impossible. Mallory and Irvine were caught in a battle against time and the unforgiving environment, with every moment a potential death sentence. As Hoyland and Moore's studies suggest, the climbers' fates were sealed not only by the sudden drop in barometric pressure but also by the cumulative toll of hypoxia, exhaustion, and exposure to the intense cold and wind. The combination of these factors, alongside the worsening weather and their limited experience with alpine survival, made any chance of survival increasingly improbable. Even if they had made it to the summit, their hopes of descending safely were dashed by the extreme conditions. The 2010 study by Moore and Semple affirms this view, concluding that the climbers' deaths were the result of a combination of physical exhaustion, hypoxia, and the insurmountable weather conditions (Hoyland; Moore, 2010).

Reconstructing Mallory and Irvine's final moments requires piecing together fragments of evidence collected over decades. The discovery of Mallory's body in 1999 provided crucial insights but also deepened the mystery. His body was found at an altitude of 27,000 feet, roughly 2,000 feet below the summit, lying face down with his arms extended above his head. The position suggested a significant fall, possibly while descending the mountain. Mallory's injuries, including a broken leg and severe head trauma, were consistent with a high-altitude fall, but the exact circumstances remain unknown.

The condition of Mallory's clothing also offered clues. Despite being exposed to the elements for 75 years, his woolen garments were remarkably well-preserved, indicating that he was well-equipped for the climb. However, the lack of modern insulation and weatherproofing likely contributed to the climbers' vulnerability. His possessions, including a pocketknife, an altimeter, and letters from Ruth, provided a poignant glimpse into his personal life but no definitive evidence of whether he reached the summit.

Expedition To The Unknown: Mallory And Irvine

The absence of Ruth's photograph, which Mallory had vowed to leave on the summit, is perhaps the most compelling detail. Some historians argue that its absence strongly suggests he placed it on the summit, fulfilling his promise. Others caution that the photograph could have been lost during the fall or removed by subsequent climbers. The discovery of Irvine's body, should it occur, may hold the key to answering this question, particularly if the Kodak camera he carried is recovered.

As with Mallory's body, the search for Irvine has spanned decades. The 1933 discovery of an ice axe, believed to belong to Irvine, provided a tantalizing clue. Found on the North Face at an altitude of approximately 27,760 feet, the axe was located along a likely descent route. This finding suggests that the duo may have been descending when tragedy struck, though whether they were descending from the summit or an aborted attempt remains unknown. Subsequent expeditions have scoured the area for Irvine's remains, but the elusive camera and other critical evidence have yet to surface.

Theories about their disappearance have evolved alongside advancements in mountaineering and forensic science. Some researchers propose that Mallory and Irvine successfully summited but were overwhelmed by the challenges of the descent, particularly as their oxygen supplies dwindled. Others argue that a fall near the Second Step, possibly during an attempt to navigate its treacherous terrain, was the decisive event. Weather conditions, equipment failures, and physical exhaustion are all factors that likely contributed to their fate.

The psychological toll of climbing in the death zone is another critical aspect of their story. At altitudes above 26,000 feet, climbers face severe cognitive impairment due to hypoxia, leading to poor decision-making and hallucinations. Mallory and Irvine, already operating at the limits of their endurance, would have been acutely vulnerable to these effects. Their ability to communicate, coordinate, and respond to unforeseen challenges would have been significantly diminished, compounding the inherent risks of the climb.

The disappearance of Mallory and Irvine and the aftermath of their ill-fated expedition continue to leave an indelible mark on the history of mountaineering and the cultural memory of Britain. Despite the absence of definitive evidence regarding their summit success, their story exemplifies the spirit of exploration and the powerful human drive to conquer the unknown. Mallory and Irvine's tragic deaths remain a poignant reminder of the extreme risks associated with such endeavors, as well as the sacrifices made in the pursuit of glory. Their climb into the death zone, undertaken with rudimentary gear and unrelenting resolve, continues to inspire climbers worldwide who are drawn to the challenge of Everest.

In the cultural and historical context of post-World War I Britain, the 1924 expedition took on additional significance. The nation, still grappling with the losses and scars of the war, looked to Everest as a symbol of resilience and national pride. The expedition was not just a quest for the summit but a search for redemption, a means of recovering a sense of purpose in a time of profound societal trauma. Mallory, Irvine, and their companions embodied this spirit of sacrifice and selflessness, reflecting the collective ethos of a generation shaped by the war. Yet, within this shared idealism, the expedition also revealed personal vulnerabilities, conflicting motivations, and the complex inner worlds of the climbers themselves.

Mallory's letters to his wife Ruth offer a glimpse into his emotional conflict – a man torn between his love for his family and his obsessive dedication to the climb. His decision to make one final attempt despite his physical limitations speaks to the depth of this internal struggle. For Irvine, the expedition was a chance to prove his worth, to transform his technical prowess into a historic achievement. The duo's partnership, forged in shared purpose, was ultimately fragile, subjected to the unforgiving conditions of the mountain. Their tragic fate also highlights the vulnerability of such partnerships in the face of nature's overwhelming power.

The immediate aftermath of the expedition was filled with uncertainty and anxiety. As the hours stretched into days without word from Mallory and Irvine, expedition leader Noel Odell, fearing the pair might be unable to locate their camp, ventured out in search of them, calling and whistling without success. The squall that had lashed the summit at around 2:00 PM finally subsided by 4:30 PM, but the weather continued to challenge the search efforts. Odell's initial optimism gave way to mounting concern, and after several fruitless days of searching, the realization set in that Mallory and Irvine were lost.

On June 10, Noel Odell, the last person to see Mallory and Irvine alive, made a final attempt to search for the missing climbers. At Camp VI, he carried two heavy sleeping bags up a snowy slope and arranged them into the shape of a large letter "T." This improvised signal was meant to communicate a devastating message to John Hazard at Camp IV: "No trace can be found, given up hope, awaiting orders." Hazard, stationed below, used blankets to replicate the signal, sending the grim update down to Camp III. There, Edward Norton and the other remaining team members responded by arranging blankets in three rows, signaling back the heartbreaking order: "Abandon search. Return as soon as possible."

The effort to maintain communication across the unforgiving terrain underscored the gravity of the situation. Each signal sent was a painful acknowledgment that the search had failed to yield any trace of Mallory and Irvine. The realization that the climbers were likely lost to the mountain struck a heavy emotional blow to the expedition. Odell's actions, hauling sleeping bags up a treacherous slope to form the signal, reflected both his dedication and his sorrow as he grappled with the reality of their disappearance. The scene at the camps was somber as the remaining expedition members came to terms with the tragedy. At Camp III, Norton and his team had hoped against hope that Mallory and Irvine might somehow return, battered but alive. When it became clear that no such miracle would occur, they began the painstaking process of packing up and preparing to descend the mountain.

In the days that followed, Odell sorted through the missing men's belongings, returning personal items such as Irvine's passport, pressure kettle, and a wallet still containing a newspaper clipping about a motorbike adventure. As the team gathered at Base Camp by June 13, a solemn cairn was constructed in honor of the twelve men lost in the three Everest expeditions, symbolizing both the sacrifice and the ultimate cost of their pursuit.

The emotional aftermath was not confined to the expedition team. Ruth Mallory, upon receiving the telegram confirming her husband's death, faced the impossible task of breaking the news to her three children. Yet, in her grief, she was determined not to overprotect them, teaching them practical skills like driving and climbing as a way to keep George's spirit alive. Ruth later reflected that "George's Spirit was ready for another life and his way of going to it was very beautiful... I know so absolutely he could not have failed in courage or self-sacrifice. If only it hadn't happened."

> *Mrs. Mallory*
> *Herschel House Cambridge*
> *Committee deeply Regret receive bad news Everest expedition today Norton cables your husband and Irvine killed last climb remainder returned safe*
> *President and committee offer you and your family heartfelt sympathy have telegraphed George's father.*

– Hinks (Arthur Hinks of the Royal Geographical Society)

For Irvine's family, the loss was equally devastating. His mother, Lilian, is said to have left a light on at the family home, waiting for his return. Although this may be a sentimental story, it reflects the deep grief that the family endured. Julie Summers recounts how Evelyn, Irvine's sister, refused to speak of her lost brother for years, while their parents silently suffered, "absolutely grief-stricken." Irvine's mother wrote to her eldest son months later, revealing that while they never questioned the rightness of Sandy's decision to climb Everest, the pain of his loss would never be healed.

The national reaction to Mallory and Irvine's deaths was one of profound shock. Mallory, as the most famous mountaineer of the time, had captured the imagination of Britain, and the loss of both climbers left the nation grieving. On June 24, King George V sent a telegram expressing his sincere sympathy to the families and the Everest Committee. The country's mourning culminated in a memorial service at St. Paul's Cathedral on October 17, 1924. The service was attended by Ruth Mallory, the parents of both climbers, members of the expedition, and representatives of the royal family, all paying tribute to the two "gallant explorers" who had given their lives in pursuit of a dream.

The tragic loss of Mallory and Irvine marked the end of the 1924 Everest expedition, but the story did not fade into obscurity. In fact, it found a new life in the form of *The Epic of Everest*, a film that would become a seminal moment in the history of mountaineering. Premiering on December 8, 1924, at London's New Scala Theatre, the film was directed by expedition member John Noel and served as a visual record of the ill-fated climb. To promote the release of the film, an extravagant event was held, featuring a stage designed to resemble a Tibetan courtyard, complete with a performance by seven monks from the Gyantse Monastery in Tibet. This performance was unlike anything London had seen before, with the monks playing cymbals, copper horns, handbells, and drums made from human skulls, along with trumpets crafted from thighbones. Their haunting Tantric chants and music served as a mystical backdrop to the film's portrayal of Everest. The monks' visit, their first time in Europe, garnered significant media attention, including several BBC radio broadcasts, further fueling the buzz around the film.

However, what began as an innovative promotional campaign soon turned into a diplomatic debacle. The event, which included the monks' ritualistic performances, was viewed as a deep affront to the Tibetan people and their culture. The spectacle stirred outrage in Tibet, where the performance of sacred music and the depiction of Tibetan adults as "savages" deeply offended both the people and the government. The outcry led to what would be known as the *Affair of the Dancing Lamas*, a scandal that ultimately resulted in the government of Tibet banning future Everest expeditions. In a letter to a British ambassador, Tibet's Prime Minister declared, "For the future, we cannot give permission to go to Tibet," effectively halting all mountaineering efforts on the world's highest peak for the next nine years.

Despite the controversy surrounding the film's promotion, the movie itself focused not on the personalities of the climbers but on the mountain itself. In Noel's eyes, Everest was the true protagonist of the expedition, its towering presence looming over the men as they made their perilous journey toward the summit. *The Epic of Everest* captured breathtaking footage of the climbers, including the haunting final images of Mallory and Irvine, two distant figures moving steadily up the unforgiving northeast ridge of Everest. These grainy, black-and-white images, shot from nearly two miles away, are some of the last known footage of the duo alive, a poignant reminder of their final, tragic ascent.

In the aftermath, however, the film's unintended diplomatic consequences reverberated far beyond the cinema. The Tibetan government's harsh reaction led to a ban on Everest expeditions, which remained in place for nearly a decade. To avoid further embarrassment, British mountaineering societies deflected blame onto John de Vars Hazard, a member of the 1924 team who had strayed from the authorized expedition route to survey the Yarlung Tsangpo River. Despite the fact that Hazard's actions were not the true cause of the diplomatic fallout, he was made the scapegoat for the next fifty years, his role in the scandal obscured from public knowledge. The legacy of Mallory and Irvine, while etched in the history of mountaineering, also became entwined with the complex political and cultural tensions of the time, ensuring that their story would live on in more ways than one.

The disappearance of Mallory and Irvine continues to captivate climbers, historians, and the broader public, fueled by tantalizing evidence and lingering questions. Their journey to the upper reaches of Everest, their determination to explore the limits of possibility, and the mystery surrounding their fate ensure that their legacy endures. Whether they reached the summit or not, Mallory and Irvine's climb represents the triumph of the human spirit and the enduring allure of the unknown.

Chapter Eight:
The Discovery of Mallory's Body in 1999

In 1999, the Mallory and Irvine Research Expedition undertook a groundbreaking mission to resolve one of mountaineering's most enduring mysteries: whether George Mallory and Andrew Irvine were the first climbers to successfully reach the summit of Mount Everest during their ill-fated 1924 expedition. This quest centered on locating Andrew Irvine's body and the Kodak camera he was believed to be carrying, which might hold photographic evidence of their achievement.

The expedition was organized by veteran Everest expedition leader Eric Simonson, with British climber Graham Hoyland as the driving force behind its initiation. A multidisciplinary team of climbers from the United States, United Kingdom, and Germany – including renowned figures like Conrad Anker, Dave Hahn, Jake Norton, Andy Politz, and Tap Richards – was assembled to execute the meticulous search. Researcher Jochen Hemmleb, who had analyzed historical records and identified a promising search area based on reports from a 1975 Chinese expedition, served as a critical advisor. The effort was financially supported by WGBH Boston's NOVA series and the BBC, further highlighting the expedition's significance.

Their search focused on a wide snow terrace at approximately 26,760 feet, situated above a steep slope leading to a 7,000-foot drop into the Rongbuk Glacier. This site, as perilous as it was expansive, offered a logical location for the remains of climbers lost in earlier attempts. However, the risks for the 1999 team were considerable. Jake Norton later reflected that even a minor misstep on the 30-degree slope could have fatal consequences.

The 1999 team was not the first to hear of potential discoveries tied to Mallory and Irvine. Chinese climbers from 1960 and 1975 had reported encountering the remains of British climbers on Everest. In 1960, Xu Jing, a member of the Chinese expedition, recounted finding a body in the Yellow Band while ascending toward Camp VII on the Northeast Ridge. Decades later, Xu elaborated on this discovery to Jochen Hemmleb and Eric Simonson after the 2001 Mallory and Irvine Research Expedition, consistently placing the body in the lee side of a dihedral, or "open book," in the Yellow Band strata. Another climber from the same expedition, Wang Fuzhou, also reported finding a corpse at approximately 8,600 meters, confidently identifying it as European due to the presence of braces on the body.

Fifteen years later, during the 1975 Chinese Everest expedition, climber Wang Hung Bao described seeing not one but possibly as many as three dead Britons within a 20-minute vicinity of Chinese Camp VI on the North Face. Wang later detailed his observation to Japanese climber Ayoten Hasegawa, noting that the body he encountered had disintegrating clothing and that its "cheeks" had been pecked by Tibetan ravens, known locally as goraks, which are common scavengers on Everest. Tragically, Wang was killed in an avalanche the following day, leaving his accounts unverified.

Adding to these discoveries were earlier sightings that predated the Chinese expeditions. In 1933, Percy Wyn-Harris stumbled upon an ice axe roughly 200 yards east of the First Step and 60 feet below the crest of the Northeast Ridge. The axe, later inspected by Noel Odell, bore three parallel nick marks that matched those on Irvine's swagger stick, discovered by his brother in 1962. This strongly suggested the axe belonged to Irvine. It remains the only concrete artifact tied to the climbers' final climb.

In 1936, British mountaineer Frank Smythe reportedly saw what he believed to be a body on the upper slopes of Everest through a high-powered telescope. In a private letter to Edward Norton, Smythe remarked that the sighting was too sensitive to disclose publicly, fearing sensationalized coverage by the press. Interestingly, Mallory's body was discovered almost exactly where Smythe had indicated seeing a figure, corroborating his account according to Graham Hoyland.

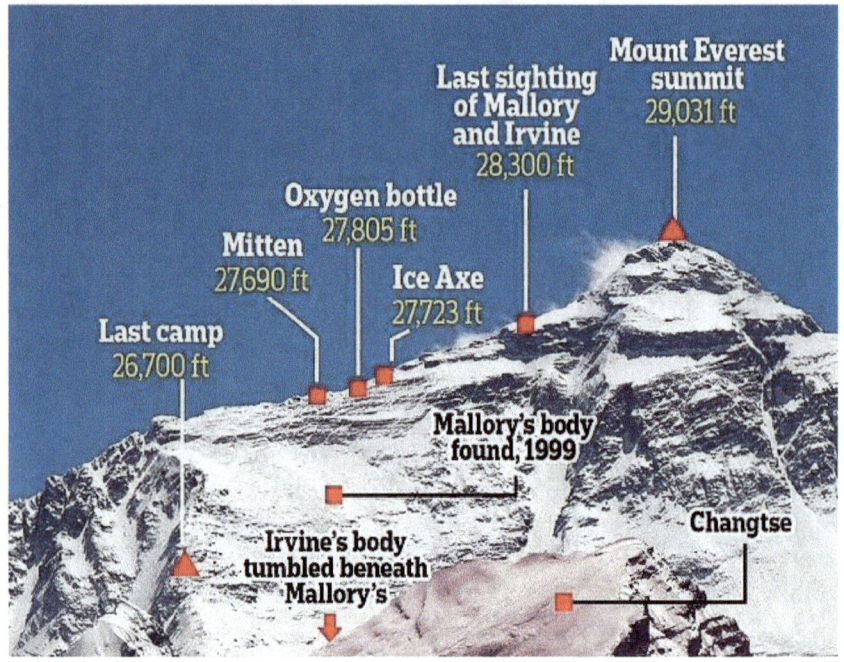

On May 1, 1999, the breakthrough moment came when Conrad Anker spotted a body protruding from the snow and ice. Using coded language to avoid alerting other teams in the area, he radioed his team with a cryptic message about a "boulder" and invited them for a "picnic." Upon arrival, the team discovered the body was remarkably well-preserved, its bleached appearance a testament to the mountain's extreme conditions. While initially thought to be Irvine, the identification was quickly confirmed: the name "G. Mallory" was stitched into the climber's clothing. (Gutosky, 2024)

Mallory's body lay face down, pointing uphill, with his upper torso fused to the scree by ice. His hobnailed boots were still intact, though his clothing had deteriorated in places. A careful examination of his remains revealed severe injuries consistent with a significant fall. His right tibia and fibula were broken, his right scapula was deformed, and his right elbow was either fractured or dislocated. Additionally, a rope encircled his torso, leaving deep bruises indicative of a fall arrested by a climbing rope. Most strikingly, a puncture wound above Mallory's left eye suggested a violent impact, possibly from his ice axe or a rock during the fall.

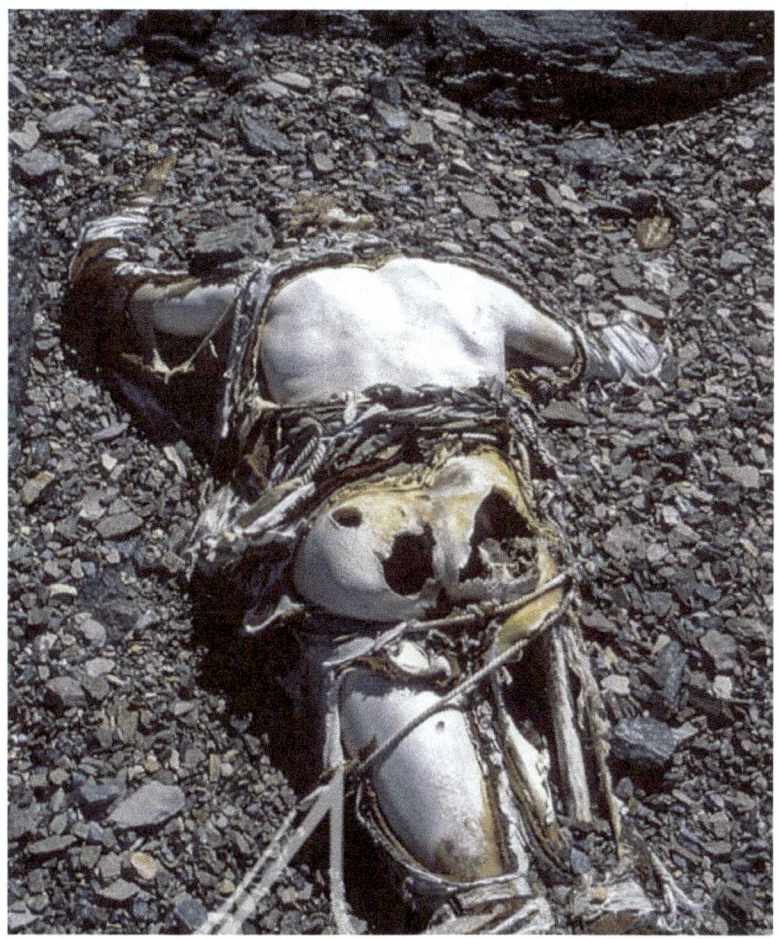

The items found on Mallory's body provided poignant and intricate insights into his final moments. Among these were personal letters, a tube of petroleum jelly wrapped in a white handkerchief, a

W.E. Oates of Sheffield manufactured Lamb foot antler-handle pocket knife encased in leather, and an intact box of Swan Vestas matches, which were still usable despite their time on the mountain. Mallory carried a variety of boot laces and straps, as well as two handkerchiefs – one with a burgundy, blue, and green foulard pattern monogrammed with "G.L.M." and another with a red, yellow, and blue pattern also bearing his initials. He also had a tin of 'Brand & Co. Savoury Meat Lozenges,' reflecting the practical preparations for sustenance on his climb.

Three letters wrapped in one of the handkerchiefs were particularly poignant: one from his brother Trafford Leigh-Mallory, another from his sister Mary Brooke, and a third from Stella Cobden-Sanderson, a supporter of the expedition. Additionally, Mallory was found with an envelope listing pressure readings for five oxygen cylinders, further evidence of his meticulous planning for the summit push.

One of the most notable discoveries was Mallory's snow goggles, which were tucked into his vest pocket. This detail strongly suggested that Mallory and Irvine were descending in darkness at the time of the accident; Mallory would not have dispensed with his goggles if he had been climbing in daylight. His wristwatch, rusted in place, displayed the time as 10 minutes past five, providing another clue to his activities on that fateful day. An altimeter was also found, though its face was broken and the hand missing, limiting its use as evidence.

However, the most sought-after artifact – the Vest Pocket Kodak camera that Mallory had allegedly borrowed from Howard Somervell – was conspicuously absent. Debate persists over whether Somervell ever gave Mallory the camera. Somervell's nephew, Jonathan Somervell, and distant relative Graham Hoyland have stated that the camera had been used by Somervell to record an image roughly 1,000 feet below the summit before he handed it off to Mallory with a fresh roll of film. Its absence remains a key unresolved element of the mystery, as it could have contained photographic proof of whether Mallory and Irvine reached the summit.

Another critical absence was the photograph of his wife, Ruth Mallory, which George had promised to leave on the summit as a symbolic gesture. Jake Norton recounted that Mallory's daughter, Claire Mallory Milliken, had shared how her mother revealed that George promised to bury a letter from her and a photograph in the summit snows. Neither the photograph nor the letter was found by the 1999 expedition or by Noel Odell during his search in 1924, further fueling speculation that Mallory may have fulfilled his promise before his tragic descent.

The team's discovery was met with profound emotion, as many of its members had grown up idolizing Mallory, viewing him as an iconic figure in mountaineering history. Mallory represented an ideal of courage, curiosity, and perseverance that resonated deeply with climbers and mountaineers for generations. For these climbers, standing before his remains was both a moment of reverence and a stark reminder of the immense sacrifices inherent in the pursuit of exploration. According to Breashears and Salkeld (1999), the team experienced a profound emotional response upon finding Mallory's body, heightened by the realization that they were in the presence of someone who had symbolized the romantic allure and tragic heroism associated with early Everest expeditions.

For Conrad Anker, the experience was deeply personal. While he had always felt uncomfortable approaching the contorted and anguished modern bodies left on Everest's slopes, Mallory's body seemed different, exuding a sense of timelessness and dignity. Tap Richards described the discovery as both awe-inspiring and sobering, reflecting on how the moment underscored the immense human cost of exploration. "After a few minutes of pictures and stunned silence, we brought ourselves around to our work. Packs and oxygen got set aside as we began to search for some identifying features and relics. I doubt that any of us this far along in our climbing and mountain careers harbored the illusion that searching the body of a dead man would be easy, but we were all a little surprised at the difficulty of our task," Richards recalled.

The body's position and injuries suggested that Mallory and Irvine had been roped together when Mallory fell, reaffirming their unbroken partnership until the moment of tragedy. This discovery dispelled speculation that one might have abandoned the other to continue alone, showing instead that they had been forcibly separated by the mountain's unforgiving conditions. The rope burns and injuries indicated Mallory's fall had been arrested by the rope before it snapped, leaving Irvine to continue the descent alone under unknown circumstances. This theory aligned with the discovery of Irvine's ice axe in 1933, marking a potential descent route.

After documenting the site, the team conducted an Anglican funeral service for Mallory, followed by covering his remains with rocks. However, on May 17, 1999, cameraman Thom Pollard and climber Andy Politz revisited the site and made additional discoveries. Using a metal detector, they located Mallory's watch and further examined his body. Pollard lifted Mallory's torso, revealing a severe head wound – a puncture above the left eye, likely caused by his ice axe or impact with a rock. Fragments of bone were visible, and dried blood confirmed the wound had occurred before death. Pollard, the only person to view Mallory's face since 1924, described him as eerily lifelike, with stubble on his chin and closed eyes, giving the impression of rest. Despite attempts to remove Mallory's leather climbing helmet for closer examination, they were unsuccessful. Politz removed Mallory's right hobnailed boot for preservation and study.

Pollard theorized that Mallory and Irvine had jettisoned their oxygen packs during their descent, as no oxygen equipment was found on Mallory. He suggested this occurred near the First Step when their oxygen had likely been depleted. The duo, burdened by exhaustion and adverse conditions, may have discarded the equipment to reduce weight, a decision tragically emblematic of their desperate struggle to survive.

Following these additional examinations, Pollard and Politz reburied Mallory's body under rocks and repeated the funeral ceremony. However, this act sparked further controversy. Critics accused the team of effectively exhuming Mallory's remains under the guise of scientific exploration. Mountaineering icons Sir Edmund Hillary and Sir Chris Bonington denounced the 1999 expedition. Hillary described the search as "distasteful," while Bonington stated, "Words can't express how disgusted I am. These people don't deserve to be called climbers." Their criticism echoed broader ethical concerns about disturbing historical remains. Mallory's grandson, also named George Mallory, expressed anger over what he perceived as disrespect, calling the handling of the expedition "bloody angry" (Macfarlane, 2012, *Into the Silence*, p. 568).

In defense of the 1999 team, it is important to note that they lacked an archaeologist among their members and were operating under extreme high-altitude conditions. While errors in judgment may have occurred, there is little evidence to suggest malice or negligence. As supporters of the expedition argue, the climbers acted to the best of their abilities in challenging circumstances, driven by a genuine desire to honor Mallory's legacy and further understanding of his final journey.

One significant artifact recovered during the expedition was Oxygen Bottle #9, found just below the First Step by Tap Richards and Jake Norton on the same day Mallory's body was discovered. This bottle had initially been spotted by Eric Simonson in 1991. Its unique valve assembly, shape, size, and stamped markings conclusively identified it as part of the 1924 British Everest Expedition. Mallory and Irvine were the only climbing party to use oxygen on that expedition, firmly linking the artifact to their summit attempt. The bottle's location, approximately 600 feet horizontally away from the top of the

First Step, further substantiated the climbers' progress along the Northeast Ridge.

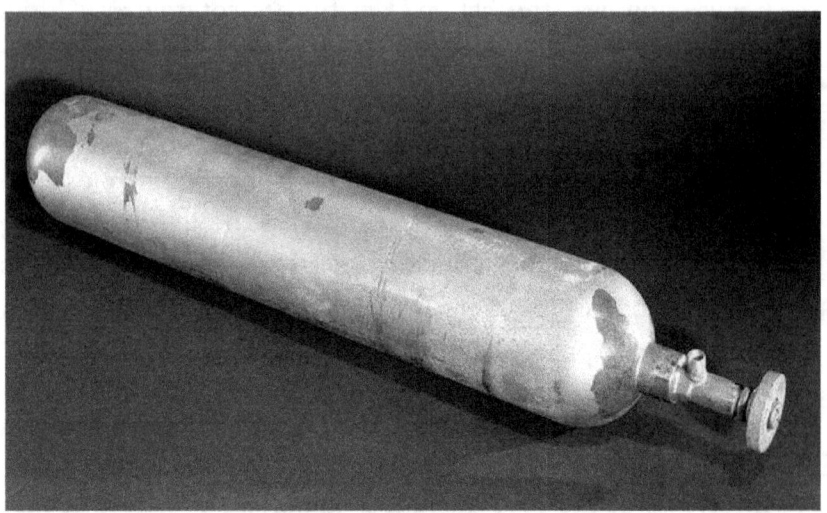

However, some ambiguity surrounds the precise recovery details. Dave Hahn, a member of the 1999 team, recalled seeing an old oxygen bottle below the exit from the Yellow Band during the ascent. A Sherpa had reportedly picked up this bottle and later cached it higher up the ridge. It remains unclear whether the bottle Hahn observed was the same as the one recovered by Richards and Norton on their descent. If the recovery site does indeed mark where the bottle was discarded in 1924, Oxygen Bottle #9 remains the highest trace of Mallory and Irvine's journey ever found. This discovery bolstered theories that they had ascended higher than previously confirmed but left unanswered the ultimate question of whether they reached the summit.

The absence of Andrew Irvine and the camera was particularly frustrating. Expedition leader Eric Simonson had prioritized the search for Irvine's body based on historical accounts from Chinese climbers who reported finding a British climber higher on the mountain. Jochen Hemmleb's analysis of these accounts had pointed the team to the area above the Yellow Band. However, Irvine's remains were not located, leaving the camera – and the potential to confirm whether Mallory and Irvine summited Everest – still buried somewhere on the unforgiving slopes. The tantalizing possibility that photographic evidence of their summit attempt existed only deepened public interest in the story.

The emotional resonance of the 1999 discovery extended beyond the technical aspects of the mystery. For the climbers who found Mallory, it was a poignant reminder of the sacrifices made by early pioneers of high-altitude exploration. Conrad Anker, who stumbled upon Mallory's body, later reflected on the profound connection he felt to the climber. "We all stand on their shoulders," he remarked, underscoring the enduring impact of Mallory and Irvine's achievements on subsequent generations of climbers.

The discovery renewed the world's focus on Mallory's legacy and highlighted the immense challenges faced by climbers during the early 20th century. The technology, clothing, and oxygen systems available to Mallory and Irvine were far less advanced than those used by modern climbers, amplifying the risks they undertook. Their woolen garments, though considered state-of-the-art at the time, offered only minimal protection against Everest's extreme cold, leaving them vulnerable to frostbite and hypothermia. Similarly, the primitive oxygen equipment they carried, prone to malfunctions and leaks, was heavy and unreliable, presenting significant logistical and survival challenges. Despite these limitations, Mallory and Irvine demonstrated extraordinary courage and resolve, embodying the indomitable spirit of exploration that continues to inspire climbers today.

The rediscovery of Mallory's body in 1999 reignited public interest in the decades-old mystery of whether Mallory and Irvine succeeded in reaching Everest's summit in 1924 before their tragic disappearance. Sir Edmund Hillary expressed deep enthusiasm about the discovery, recognizing its historical significance and Mallory's foundational role in Everest exploration. "He was really the initial pioneer of the whole idea of climbing Mount Everest," Hillary remarked. However, Mallory's son, John, offered a more tempered perspective, asserting, "To me, the only way you achieve a summit is to come back alive; the job's half done if you don't get down again." This view underscored the harsh realities of high-altitude climbing, where survival is the ultimate measure of success.

The renewed interest also brought attention to Andrew Irvine, whose contributions to the expedition have often been overshadowed by Mallory's towering legacy. Irvine's mechanical expertise with the oxygen apparatus was instrumental in enabling the pair to attempt the summit, despite his relative inexperience as a climber. His presence on the expedition reflected remarkable determination and courage. The hope of finding Irvine's body – and the Kodak camera he was believed to carry – remains a driving force behind continued searches on Everest, as it could hold photographic evidence of whether the duo reached the summit (Ortner, 2001).

The rediscovery of Mallory's body spurred subsequent expeditions aimed at locating Irvine and solving the enduring mystery once and for all. One such expedition in 2001 revisited areas identified during the 1999 search but was again unsuccessful in locating Irvine's remains or the elusive camera. Technological advancements in imaging and forensic analysis have since raised hopes that future efforts might finally yield answers. However, the challenges of operating in Everest's extreme environment – compounded by shifting ice, snow, and the unpredictable nature of the mountain – make such endeavors exceedingly difficult (Broughton, 2002).

The discovery also provided an opportunity for reflection on Everest's broader historical and cultural legacy. During the 1999 expedition, Conrad Anker and Dave Hahn reached the summit of Everest on May 17th at 2:50 p.m., highlighting the stark contrast between modern climbing capabilities and the early efforts of pioneers like Mallory and Irvine. While modern climbers benefit from advanced equipment, fixed ropes, and well-established routes, the courage and determination of the early explorers continue to be a source of admiration and respect.

The impact of the discovery also resonated in academic and cultural circles. Historians and mountaineers alike revisited the details of the 1924 expedition, analyzing diaries, letters, and other artifacts to gain a deeper understanding of Mallory and Irvine's motivations and challenges. Biographers revisited Mallory's life, exploring his philosophy of climbing and his famous declaration that Everest must be climbed "because it's there."

For climbers, Mallory's rediscovery was both an inspiration and a cautionary tale. His story serves as a reminder of the importance of preparation, teamwork, and respect for the mountain. At the same time, it underscores the allure of pushing the boundaries of human achievement, even in the face of overwhelming odds. As historian Peter Hansen (2000) notes, Mallory's tragic end speaks to the existential risks that early explorers willingly faced in their quests for discovery, which, in turn, underscored the human cost associated with exploration during this period. Modern expeditions to Everest often pay homage to Mallory and Irvine, viewing their efforts as a foundation for the successes of future generations.

The personal significance of Mallory's death resonates deeply, particularly through the letters and artifacts recovered with his body. His correspondence with his wife, Ruth, reveals a man torn between his love for his family and his relentless drive to achieve greatness. Mallory's promise to leave Ruth's photograph on the summit has become a symbol of his determination, as well as the personal sacrifices inherent in such ambitious pursuits.

As interest in the Mallory-Irvine mystery endures, so does the broader legacy of their expedition. It serves as a testament to the resilience of the human spirit and the unyielding drive to explore, understand, and achieve. Their story continues to inspire climbers, historians, and adventurers, ensuring that their names remain synonymous with the pursuit of the impossible. This lasting legacy underscores the cultural impact of Mallory's life and death, illustrating how the memory of explorers is often reshaped by later discoveries and shifting public perceptions (Salkeld & Boyle, 1999).

Chapter Nine: The Search for Andrew Irvine

The search for Andrew Irvine has continued for a century, driven by the enduring mystery of whether he and George Mallory reached the summit of Everest before their tragic disappearance in 1924. While the discovery of Mallory's body in 1999 provided some answers, it left one of the most critical questions unresolved: where was Irvine? Many have speculated that uncovering his remains – and more importantly, the Kodak camera he was believed to be carrying – could finally reveal the truth about their final climb. As the decades have passed, mountaineers, historians, and explorers have been relentless in their pursuit of evidence, using both traditional climbing techniques and modern technology to search for traces of Irvine high on Everest's treacherous slopes.

In 2024, that search took a historic turn. What had once seemed an insurmountable mystery was suddenly within reach when a team led by climber and filmmaker Jimmy Chin made a discovery that shocked the mountaineering world. While descending the Central Rongbuk Glacier after a ski descent of the Hornbein Couloir, Chin and his team were not actively searching for Irvine. Their focus had been on a groundbreaking ski expedition, yet fate had other plans. Several hundred feet below where Mallory's remains had been discovered, something unexpected emerged from the ice – a boot, weathered with age, its leather brittle and worn by time. The hobnailed sole bore a diamond-patterned steel design unmistakably belonging to a climber from the early 20th century. Upon closer inspection, the boot was found to contain a foot, still clad in a sock bearing a name tag: A. C. IRVINE.

It was a discovery that carried immense significance. For years, theories about Irvine's whereabouts had ranged from claims that his body had been hidden by the Chinese in 1975 to speculation that he had fallen to a remote and unreachable crevasse. The find immediately set off a wave of speculation about what might still be hidden beneath the ice. If his foot had surfaced, then was the rest of his body nearby? And more importantly, could the long-lost Kodak camera be recovered with it?

Before finding Irvine's boot, Chin's team had already made a notable discovery – a 1933 oxygen cylinder. This was significant in its own right, as the 1933 British Everest expedition had previously found Irvine's ice axe in the vicinity of the First Step. The presence of an oxygen bottle from that same year prompted Chin and his team to reconsider their surroundings. If an oxygen bottle could have tumbled so far down, then what of a human body? A body would not have moved as freely as a lightweight piece of metal. Its trajectory would have been slower, potentially stopping along the way or becoming caught in glacial ice for decades. Chin hypothesized that if the bottle had reached this point, then Irvine's remains might not be far away.

The moment of discovery was nothing short of surreal. As the team carefully navigated the glacier's crevasses and ridges, they spotted the boot protruding from the ice. The weight of history was not lost on them. "I think it literally melted out a week before we found it," Chin later reflected. The implications of this discovery were monumental, not just for historians and climbers but for Irvine's family, who had spent a century waiting for answers.

Efforts to locate Irvine had been extensive over the years. Dozens of expeditions had scoured the North Face of Everest in search of him, each one returning empty-handed. Chinese climbers in the 1960s and 1970s had reported seeing bodies high on the mountain, but none had been positively identified as Irvine. Theories flourished. Some believed that the Chinese had secretly removed Irvine's remains to protect their claim that the first successful summit via the North Ridge had been made by a Chinese team in 1960. Others speculated that Irvine's body had long since been buried under deep layers of ice, never to be found. The revelation that at least part of his remains had been carried by the glacier confirmed that his body had not been removed in secret – it had simply been shifting with the mountain's natural forces.

The condition of the foot suggested a violent end. Edwards theorized that if Irvine had fallen a great distance, his body may have shattered upon impact, breaking apart as it tumbled over the mountain's rock-strewn terrain. This could explain why only a portion of his remains had been recovered so far. Edwards pointed out that if Irvine's body had indeed been seen high on the mountain in 1960, then he must have died during his descent, not on the way up. If he had become immobilized due to exhaustion or injury, Mallory may have been forced to leave him behind in an attempt to reach Camp V and get help. Mallory's body was later found along a line leading toward Camp V, suggesting that he had been descending with urgency. This would mean that Irvine's final moments were spent alone, stranded high on Everest, before his body was later swept away by an avalanche or other natural forces.

Conrad Anker, who had discovered Mallory's body in 1999, offered his own perspective on Irvine's fate. He believed that the simplest explanation was likely the correct one. "On June 8, 1924, Mallory's body came to a stop, and Irvine's kept going," he suggested. "I think he was swept off the mountain." If this theory holds true, then

Irvine's camera, if he was indeed carrying it, might have been lost along with his body, potentially shattered beyond recognition. But until the rest of Irvine's remains are recovered, there remains hope that the camera – or at least some of his personal effects – might still be intact.

The China Tibet Mountaineering Association has since taken possession of Irvine's remains, ensuring that the discovery is treated with the respect it deserves. The finding has been reported to the Royal Geographical Society, which had originally organized the 1924 expedition, as well as to the Alpine Club. The question of whether the missing camera will be found remains unanswered, but for the first time in a century, there is reason to believe that the truth about Mallory and Irvine's final climb may finally be within reach.

The implications of this discovery stretch far beyond the recovery of a lost climber. Historians have long argued that finding Irvine might solve the debate over whether Mallory and Irvine reached the summit before their deaths. Many believe that Irvine was carrying the Kodak Vest Pocket camera, which, if recovered and its film developed, could confirm or refute their success.

According to Everest historian Jochen Hemmleb, the location of the discovery opens up several possibilities for how Irvine's body reached the glacier. He suggests that Irvine may have fallen from the Northeast Ridge, been swept down by an avalanche from the north face, or even been thrown from the mountain by the force of a fall. Dr. Robert Edwards, a glaciologist, examined the discovery and concluded that Irvine's remains had been transported over time by the slow movement of the Central Rongbuk Glacier. He proposed two possible explanations for how Irvine's foot ended up at this location. One scenario suggests that Irvine fell all the way down the mountain on June 8, 1924, and his body was gradually carried by the glacier over the past century. The second theory posits that Irvine initially perished higher on the mountain – perhaps near the 8,600-meter location where Wang Fuzhou claimed to have seen a body in 1960. If this were the case, his remains may have remained intact on the slopes of Everest for decades before finally succumbing to gravity or an avalanche, sending them tumbling to the head of the glacier, where they were then transported between one and three kilometers from their original location (Dr. Robert Edwards, 2024).

Edwards also theorizes that Irvine's descent may have been violent, causing his body to shatter upon impact as it fell over Everest's unforgiving rock faces. The fact that only a portion of his remains have surfaced suggests that the rest of his body may have broken apart or become buried deeper within the glacier. This aligns with occasional reports from past expeditions of unidentified skeletal remains that may have belonged to early Everest climbers. If Irvine's body was indeed seen high on the mountain in 1960, then this would indicate that he initially perished in a relatively intact state before being dislodged years later. If true, this theory adds weight to the idea that Mallory may have left him behind, potentially injured or exhausted, while attempting to descend to Camp V for help.

The 2024 discovery also raises questions about previous claims regarding Irvine's remains. In 1975, Chinese climber Wang Hung Bao reported seeing multiple British bodies near Chinese Camp VI, but he was killed in an avalanche the next day before he could provide further details. Mark Synnott, an Everest historian, has argued that the Chinese removed Irvine's body and camera in 1975 to protect their claim that the 1960 Chinese expedition was the first successful ascent of Everest's North Ridge. This theory is based on a 1984 account from a British diplomat in Beijing, who was reportedly told by Chinese mountaineer Pan Dou that Irvine's body had been found at 8,200 meters. According to Pan Dou, the Chinese team attempted to develop the film from the camera but were unsuccessful. However, the 2024 discovery of Irvine's foot on the glacier challenges this theory. If Irvine's body was taken down by the Chinese in 1975, how did part of him end up encased in ice further down the glacier decades later? Hemmleb argues that while the discovery is significant, it does not entirely rule out all theories about Irvine's fate, except for the claim that his body was secretly transported to Lhasa, which can now be definitively dismissed (Hemmleb, 2024).

If the discovery of Irvine's remains can be conclusively verified, it will not only be a historic moment in mountaineering but also a deeply personal one for Irvine's family. His great-niece, Julie Summers, has dedicated much of her career to preserving his memory and uncovering the truth about his disappearance. The Irvine family has offered to provide DNA for testing to confirm the identity of the remains, an unprecedented step that could finally bring closure to a century-old mystery. Summers, upon learning of the discovery, described being moved to tears by the realization that a piece of her great-uncle had finally returned to history. "It's an object that belonged to him and has a bit of him in it," she said. "It tells the whole story about what probably happened" (Summers, 2024).

The discovery also reignites discussions about Irvine's legacy and how it differs from Mallory's. At just 22 years old, Irvine was significantly younger than Mallory, who at 37 was a seasoned mountaineer with decades of experience. While Mallory was revered as one of the finest rock climbers of his generation, Irvine had little formal climbing experience. His selection as Mallory's climbing partner has long been debated, as many historians have argued that Mallory might have chosen a more experienced climber. However, letters uncovered in 2020 suggest that Mallory had identified Irvine as his preferred partner as early as April 1924. Irvine himself wrote to his mother on April 24, stating, "I have provisionally been chosen to do the first oxygen climb with Mallory. Norton & Somervell doing non-ox on same day. It will be great fun if we all 4 get to the top at the same time!" His letter conveys a youthful enthusiasm that stands in stark contrast to the gravity of the mission ahead. It also underscores Mallory's confidence in him, despite Irvine's limited high-altitude experience (Summers, 2020).

Irvine's primary role on the expedition was as a technical expert, particularly in maintaining and repairing the expedition's oxygen apparatus. Unlike Mallory, who was known for his poetic musings on climbing, Irvine was a pragmatic and methodical problem-solver. His mechanical skills made him an asset to the team, and some historians believe that his expertise with the oxygen equipment was a deciding factor in Mallory's choice of him as a partner. This distinction between the two climbers has shaped how history remembers them. Mallory is often portrayed as the romantic idealist, driven by a philosophical desire to conquer Everest "because it's there." Irvine, on the other hand, is remembered more as a young and capable engineer, whose contributions were essential but whose legacy has remained overshadowed by Mallory's.

With the recent discovery of his remains, Irvine has, at last, stepped out from Mallory's shadow. His name is no longer just an afterthought in one of mountaineering's greatest mysteries but a focal point of renewed interest and research. The questions that remain – where the rest of his body is, whether the camera will ever be found, and what new insights this discovery will yield – are now at the center of Everest exploration. For the first time in a century, the story of Andrew Irvine is being told on its own terms.

The allure of this mystery lies not only in its historical significance but also in the emotional and philosophical questions it raises. Would definitive proof that Mallory and Irvine summited Everest before their deaths change the way their legacy is perceived? Would it rewrite the history of Everest's first ascent, currently credited to Sir Edmund Hillary and Tenzing Norgay in 1953? Some argue that it would be merely a footnote in the grander history of mountaineering, as true success on Everest is defined not only by reaching the summit but by returning safely. John Mallory, George Mallory's son, famously stated, "To me, the only way you achieve a summit is to come back alive; the job's half done if you don't get down again" (Summers, 2024). His words reflect the pragmatic reality of high-altitude exploration, where survival is the ultimate test of a climber's skill and endurance.

Despite this perspective, the desire to know the truth persists. However, the mountain remains an unpredictable and unforgiving place. Some historians, including Jochen Hemmleb, have cautioned that even if Irvine's body is fully recovered, the camera – if it was with him – may have been lost or damaged beyond recognition. The harsh environment of Everest, with its extreme cold, moisture, and high winds, is unlikely to have preserved film in a recoverable state. Yet, the hope remains, and the search continues (Hemmleb, 2024).

For Irvine's family, the mystery has been both a source of pride and pain. His relatives have long supported the ongoing search for his remains, believing that solving the mystery could provide long-awaited closure. The emotional weight of Irvine's disappearance has lingered through generations, shaping the way his family has remembered and honored him. Unlike Mallory, whose widow, Ruth, played an active role in curating his posthumous legacy, the Irvine family has largely maintained a more private approach. However, in recent years, his great-niece has become an outspoken advocate for preserving his story and ensuring that his contributions to the 1924 expedition are fully recognized.

Summers recalls being moved to tears when she received the phone call from Jimmy Chin confirming the discovery of Irvine's boot. The find was deeply personal for her, as it was not just an artifact of mountaineering history but a tangible piece of the uncle her family had mourned for generations. "It's an object that belonged to him and has a bit of him in it," she said. "It tells the whole story about what probably happened" (Summers, 2024). She has since expressed hope that the remains will undergo DNA testing to confirm Irvine's identity and that further searches may recover more of his body. However, she also acknowledges the likelihood that Irvine's body may have been broken apart by the mountain's harsh conditions and the movement of the glacier over the past century.

The Irvine family's private grief contrasts with the public fascination surrounding the mystery. Some historians have suggested that the romanticization of Everest's early explorers has overshadowed the real human cost of these expeditions. Andrew Irvine was just 22 years old when he disappeared, a young man with his entire life ahead of him. Unlike Mallory, who was already an established mountaineering figure, Irvine was still finding his place in the world. His selection for the 1924 expedition, despite his limited climbing experience, was due to his mechanical skills, which made him invaluable in maintaining the team's oxygen equipment. This distinction between the two men – Mallory as the visionary and Irvine as the pragmatic engineer – has influenced the way they are remembered. While Mallory is often depicted as the tragic hero, Irvine is remembered as the bright but inexperienced young man who accompanied him, a characterization that overlooks the courage and determination he displayed in undertaking such a perilous climb (Holzel & Salkeld, 1999; Conefrey, 2012).

Julie Summers has worked to shift this narrative, emphasizing that Irvine was not merely a supporting figure but a crucial part of the expedition. Letters and documents uncovered in recent years reveal that Mallory had identified Irvine as his preferred climbing partner long before their final ascent. In his letter to his mother, Irvine expressed enthusiasm about being chosen to climb with Mallory, demonstrating that he saw himself as an active participant rather than a passive companion (Summers, 2020).

The toll of Irvine's loss on his family was profound. Stories persist that for years after his disappearance, his mother, Lilian, left a light on and the door unlocked at their home in Birkenhead, hoping that one day her son would return. Whether fact or legend, the story captures the deep sorrow and unfulfilled hope that accompanied his absence. His sister, Evelyn, reportedly kept a photo of him by her bedside until the day she died, describing him as "a better man than anyone would ever be" (Summers, 2024). Unlike many wartime losses of the era, where families at least had the solace of a known burial site, Irvine's disappearance left his relatives with nothing but unanswered questions.

This lack of closure is part of what continues to make Irvine's story so compelling to modern audiences. His remains, scattered by the forces of nature, symbolize the unpredictability and unforgiving nature of Everest. His youth and potential, cut short at the beginning of a promising life, resonate with those who see him not just as a historical figure but as a person who never had the chance to grow old. Some have even drawn comparisons to figures like John F. Kennedy or James Dean – icons who remain forever young in the public imagination. The image of Irvine as the eager, ambitious young climber contrasts sharply with Mallory's established legacy, reinforcing the idea that he was a figure of untapped potential rather than a fully realized mountaineering legend (Davis, 2020).

The impact of this discovery extends beyond the realm of mountaineering. It is a reminder of the human cost of exploration, of the families left behind, and of the mysteries that endure long after the climbers themselves have vanished. Whether or not the final answers ever emerge, Irvine's story will continue to inspire those who seek adventure and those who strive to uncover the past. His name, once relegated to the background of Mallory's tale, is now spoken with equal reverence, ensuring that his place in history is finally recognized.

Tyler Long

Chapter Ten: *The Legacy of Mallory and Irvine – Mountaineering's Greatest Mystery*

Mallory and Irvine's influence on modern mountaineering is undeniable. Their ill-fated 1924 attempt to summit Everest stands as a pivotal moment in the history of high-altitude climbing, shaping the culture, technology, and ethical considerations of mountaineering for a century. Their expedition is often viewed as a defining example of human ambition, perseverance, and the pursuit of the unknown. The legacy they left behind has inspired generations of climbers, reinforcing the idea that the journey itself can be just as important as the destination. Mallory's famous declaration, "Because it is there," remains one of the most enduring quotes in exploration history, capturing the romantic ideal of adventure. The philosophical divide between exploration for its own sake and the structured, methodical approach to climbing that emerged in later decades can be seen in the contrast between Mallory and Irvine's climb and the successful ascent of Everest by Edmund Hillary and Tenzing Norgay in 1953 (Holzel & Salkeld, 1996).

***

The 1953 British Mount Everest expedition was the ninth organized attempt to conquer the world's highest peak and the first to achieve confirmed success. Edmund Hillary of New Zealand and Tenzing Norgay of Nepal reached the summit on May 29, 1953, marking a historic milestone in mountaineering. The expedition, meticulously planned and led by Colonel John Hunt, was backed by the Joint Himalayan Committee, a collaboration between the Alpine Club and the Royal Geographical Society. The news of their triumph was strategically announced on June 2, coinciding with the coronation of Queen Elizabeth II, thus amplifying its national and symbolic significance.

John Hunt's appointment as leader came as a surprise to many, as Eric Shipton had long been considered the natural choice. Shipton, a seasoned mountaineer, had led the crucial 1951 reconnaissance expedition and was highly respected among his peers. However, the committee ultimately chose Hunt due to his extensive military leadership experience, believing he could better orchestrate a large-scale effort to finally reach the summit. This decision was not without controversy. Several climbers loyal to Shipton expressed their dissatisfaction, with Charles Evans remarking that "it was said that Shipton lacked the killer instinct – not a bad thing to lack in my view." Even Hillary initially opposed Hunt's appointment but was eventually convinced of his capabilities. George Band later reflected that while the decision to replace Shipton may have been strategically sound, its execution was handled poorly, leading to tension within the team.

Despite the initial controversy, Hunt's leadership proved effective, and the team assembled for the expedition was exceptionally skilled. Edmund Hillary, a 34-year-old New Zealand beekeeper, had honed his mountaineering abilities in the challenging New Zealand Alps, where he had also pioneered winter ski mountaineering. A veteran of the Royal New Zealand Air Force during World War II, his technical expertise and physical endurance made him an ideal candidate. Tenzing Norgay, the 39-year-old Sherpa leader, was the most experienced Everest climber of his time. Having participated in numerous previous expeditions, including the near-successful Swiss attempt in 1952, his knowledge of the mountain was invaluable. Their partnership, forged in the Himalayas, would prove instrumental in the expedition's ultimate success.

The expedition took the South Col route from Nepal, an approach first explored by Eric Shipton in 1951 and later tested by the Swiss in 1952. Prior to this, British expeditions had traditionally approached Everest from the Tibetan side, but political changes following China's occupation of Tibet forced a shift in strategy. The South Col route was deemed promising, given that Tenzing and Swiss climber Raymond Lambert had reached an altitude of 28,200 feet – just 800 feet below the summit – during their attempt the previous year. Hunt's team carefully built upon the knowledge gained from these previous expeditions, determined to succeed where others had fallen short.

The team departed Kathmandu on March 10, 1953, accompanied by 362 porters, 20 Sherpa guides, and over 10,000 pounds of equipment. After a grueling 170-mile trek, they arrived at Namche Bazaar on March 25 and began their ascent toward Base Camp, which was established at 18,000 feet on the Khumbu Glacier. The route required navigating several key obstacles, including the treacherous Khumbu Icefall and the Western Cwm, a vast, sheltered basin where they set up Camp IV at 23,000 feet. Progressing further, the team established Camp V near the base of the Lhotse Face and Camp VI on the South Col at 26,000 feet. The final high-altitude camps, Camp VII and Camp VIII, were positioned at 27,500 feet, serving as the launch points for the summit attempts.

Hunt's strategy involved three summit attempts, each consisting of two climbers. The first attempt, undertaken by Tom Bourdillon and Charles Evans, aimed to reach the South Summit and, if possible, continue to the main summit. This team used an experimental closed-circuit oxygen system, which, despite being highly efficient, proved unreliable. They reached the South Summit on May 26 but were forced to turn back due to oxygen system failures and exhaustion. The second attempt, led by Hillary and Tenzing using open-circuit oxygen systems, was scheduled next. If their attempt failed, Wilfrid Noyce and Mike Ward were prepared to launch a final assault following a recovery period to replenish high-altitude supplies.

The team relied on two types of oxygen apparatus: a closed-circuit system, which provided 100 percent oxygen directly from the cylinder, and an open-circuit system, which mixed oxygen with fresh air. The closed-circuit system, while efficient, was heavier and prone to technical issues. The open-circuit system, used by Hillary and Tenzing, was more practical, allowing for sustained performance at extreme altitudes. In addition to improved oxygen systems, the climbers were equipped with specialized high-altitude clothing, including windproof cotton suits, insulated nylon trousers, and lightweight jerseys. Their boots were designed to prevent slippage on ice, while their gloves consisted of close-fitting silk liners beneath windproof cotton gauntlets for optimal dexterity and protection.

On May 27, 1953, Hillary and Tenzing set out from Camp IX at 6:30 a.m., following the South Col route. The first 500 feet of ascent was slow but steady. As they approached the South Summit, they encountered a dangerously unstable 400-foot snow face. Hillary later recalled, "Not only was it very steep, but the snow was, I felt, in a dangerous condition. Laboriously beating a track up it – sometimes up to our knees and often deeper – we were always conscious of the tremendous drop to the Kangshung Glacier, 11,000 feet below us." Tenzing, though apprehensive, trusted Hillary's judgment, and they continued. After reaching the South Summit at 9:00 a.m., they assessed their oxygen supply and determined they had roughly four and a half hours remaining for the final push.

The final ascent involved traversing treacherous ridges flanked by cornices and deep drop-offs. Progress required meticulous step-cutting and careful belaying. The most formidable obstacle was a steep rock bluff that appeared nearly impassable. Hillary identified a narrow gap between the ice and rock, using his crampons for traction while leveraging his hands against the rock. With Tenzing's assistance, he maneuvered through the gap and pulled his partner up beside him. The final section consisted of a series of corniced ridges, and after nearly two hours of grueling effort, they reached the summit at 11:30 a.m.

At the highest point on Earth, Hillary and Tenzing took a moment to document their success, burying a small cross and some sweets in the snow. Hillary briefly removed his oxygen mask to take photographs but quickly noticed the onset of clumsiness due to the lack of oxygen. They spent roughly 15 minutes on the summit before beginning their descent. Upon reuniting with George Lowe at Camp IV, Hillary made his now-famous understated remark: "Well, George, we knocked the bastard off."

The expedition's filmmaker, Tom Stobart, had instructed Hillary and Tenzing to withhold the news of their success until it could be captured on film at Base Camp. This calculated delay allowed Stobart to document the team's authentic reactions upon receiving confirmation that Everest had been conquered.

The 1953 expedition remains one of the greatest milestones in mountaineering history. It was a triumph of human endurance, teamwork, and strategic planning. The verified ascent of Hillary and Tenzing contrasts sharply with the lingering mystery of Mallory and Irvine's 1924 attempt. The South Col route, chosen for its relative feasibility, proved to be a more practical approach than the technically demanding Northeast Ridge attempted by Mallory and Irvine. With superior oxygen systems, insulated gear, and carefully planned logistics, the 1953 expedition had significant advantages over the 1924 effort. Yet, despite these advancements, Everest remained an unforgiving challenge, and the achievement of Hillary and Tenzing was a testament to the evolution of high-altitude mountaineering (Holzel & Salkeld, 1999; Hillary, 1955).

***

The 1924 expedition took place in an era when mountaineering was as much a test of character and fortitude as it was of physical ability. Mallory and Irvine embodied the spirit of early 20th-century exploration, when great expeditions were seen as national endeavors, driven by the idea of proving human resilience in the face of extreme challenges. Their disappearance near the summit of Everest elevated them from mere climbers to mythic figures, forever linked to the mountain they sought to conquer. In contrast, the 1953 expedition represented a turning point in the way Everest was approached. Hillary and Norgay's ascent was the result of meticulous planning, technological advancements, and a deeper understanding of the mountain's conditions. Their success marked the beginning of modern high-altitude climbing, where logistical precision and technological support played a crucial role in summiting Everest. While Mallory and Irvine relied on instinct, endurance, and rudimentary equipment, later climbers benefited from improved gear, better oxygen systems, and carefully coordinated strategies (Salkeld, 1996). Even though it does not pertain directly to Mallory and Irvine, the 1953 ascent holds significant relevance to their legacy. It provided the first indisputable proof that Everest could be climbed, solidifying the mountain as an achievable feat rather than an unattainable dream. At the same time, it reignited the debate over whether the true first ascent had occurred in 1924, ensuring that the mystery of Mallory and Irvine's fate would remain a central and contested topic in mountaineering history.

One of the most significant ways in which Mallory and Irvine's climb influenced modern mountaineering was through the evolution of climbing technology. Their expedition exposed the limitations of early high-altitude gear, paving the way for innovations that would transform the sport. The woolen clothing, hobnailed boots, and basic ice axes they used were state-of-the-art at the time but inadequate for the extreme conditions of Everest. Their oxygen systems, though groundbreaking, were unreliable and cumbersome, leading some members of the expedition to forego them entirely. The weaknesses in their equipment highlighted the need for better solutions, driving future developments in mountaineering technology. Over time, synthetic materials replaced natural fibers, allowing climbers to remain warm while reducing weight. Insulated, waterproof boots with integrated crampons vastly improved stability and traction on ice. Ice axes, once simple tools for balance and self-arrest, evolved into highly specialized implements designed for technical climbing.

Perhaps the most critical advancement spurred by the early Everest expeditions was in the development of high-altitude oxygen systems. The closed-circuit oxygen apparatus used in 1924 provided a continuous supply of oxygen but was inefficient and prone to failure. By 1953, climbers had access to more effective open-circuit systems, which mixed pure oxygen with fresh air, increasing efficiency and ease of use. Modern climbers now benefit from lightweight oxygen cylinders, advanced regulators, and improved delivery systems that optimize oxygen intake at extreme altitudes (Salkeld, 2003). These advancements have dramatically increased the chances of survival and success on Everest, allowing climbers to function more effectively in the death zone above 26,000 feet.

Climbing techniques have also undergone a radical transformation since 1924. Mallory and Irvine relied on step-cutting, a physically demanding and time-consuming method that involved carving footholds into the ice with an axe. Today, climbers use fixed ropes, harnesses, and carabiners to ascend steep sections with greater safety and efficiency. Navigation has also improved significantly. Where Mallory and Irvine relied on barometric altimeters and compass readings, modern climbers use GPS devices, satellite communication, and detailed weather forecasting to plan their routes. These advancements have made Everest more accessible, reducing the number of unknowns that early climbers had to contend with.

While the technological progress inspired by Mallory and Irvine's climb has made Everest more attainable, it has also raised ethical questions about modern high-altitude mountaineering. Their era was one of pure exploration, where climbers faced the mountain with little external assistance. Today, Everest has become a commercialized endeavor, with guided expeditions offering climbers the chance to reach the summit for a steep fee, regardless of experience. This shift has led to overcrowding, increased fatalities, and concerns about the environmental impact of mass tourism on the mountain. The debate over what constitutes a "true" ascent has intensified, with some arguing that modern Everest expeditions, reliant on Sherpa support and fixed infrastructure, diminish the challenge that pioneers like Mallory and Irvine faced. Others contend that technology and commercialization have democratized mountaineering, making Everest accessible to a wider range of climbers while improving safety standards.

Another significant ethical issue that has come to the forefront is the role of Sherpas in high-altitude mountaineering. In 1924, Sherpa contributions were largely overlooked, with British climbers receiving the majority of the credit for expedition successes. The 1953 ascent of Everest helped change this perception, as Tenzing Norgay was rightly recognized as an equal partner in the summit achievement. However, the modern climbing industry has placed an even greater burden on Sherpas, who are often required to take on the most dangerous tasks, including fixing ropes, carrying heavy loads, and rescuing stranded climbers. The commercialization of Everest has led to debates about fair wages, working conditions, and the ethical responsibilities of foreign climbers toward their Sherpa teams (Ortner, 1999).

Expedition To The Unknown: Mallory And Irvine

Mallory and Irvine's climb serves as both an inspiration and a cautionary tale in this ongoing ethical debate. Their approach to Everest, though deeply flawed in terms of technology and strategy, was built on personal determination and a willingness to embrace risk. They were not reliant on the extensive support systems that exist today, nor did they have the luxury of detailed weather forecasts, high-altitude porters, or pre-established routes. Their attempt represents a purer, albeit more perilous, form of exploration – one that continues to be revered by those who value self-sufficiency in the mountains. At the same time, their story is a reminder of the inherent dangers of high-altitude climbing and the thin line between ambition and recklessness.

The legacy of Mallory and Irvine extends far beyond the unanswered question of whether they reached the summit. Their expedition set the stage for a century of innovation in mountaineering, influencing the development of equipment, climbing techniques, and ethical standards. Their climb continues to inspire those who seek to push the limits of human endurance, while also prompting reflection on the changing nature of Everest itself. As modern climbers ascend the world's highest peak with the aid of advanced technology and commercial guiding services, Mallory and Irvine's story remains a powerful reminder of the raw, unfiltered challenge that Everest once posed.

Like other pioneers lost in the pursuit of discovery, such as Amelia Earhart or Robert Falcon Scott, they have become symbols of human ambition, courage, and tragedy. Their story is unique because of the lingering mystery surrounding their final hours. While Scott's ill-fated Antarctic expedition was well-documented, and Earhart's disappearance over the Pacific left only speculation, Mallory and Irvine exist in a space between the known and the unknown. The possibility that they reached the summit before perishing has transformed them into enduring cultural icons. Had they returned safely, they would have been celebrated as heroes, but their legend would not have carried the same weight. The uncertainty of their fate has kept them at the forefront of mountaineering lore for a century, inspiring generations of climbers, writers, and historians to piece together the final moments of their ascent.

The tragic element of their story is further amplified by the notion that they remain forever young. Unlike climbers who lived long enough to see their achievements recognized, Mallory and Irvine's untimely deaths have frozen them in time, much like James Dean, John F. Kennedy, or Marilyn Monroe. The world never saw them grow old, and in this way, they exist eternally as ambitious, daring figures, forever locked in their final attempt on Everest. This sense of eternal youth, combined with the mystery surrounding their disappearance, has contributed to their mythic status. They embody the archetype of explorers who sacrificed everything in the pursuit of the unknown, becoming larger-than-life figures in the process.

Mallory's fixation on Everest was undeniable. His participation in the British expeditions of 1921, 1922, and 1924 demonstrates an obsessive commitment to reaching the summit. The phrase "Summit Fever" describes the psychological drive that pushes climbers beyond rational decision-making, often at great personal risk. While the term is commonly applied to modern climbers who ignore warning signs in their quest to reach the top, some have speculated that Mallory's unrelenting pursuit of Everest may have been an early example of this phenomenon. His repeated attempts, despite the immense dangers and failures of previous expeditions, suggest that Everest had become more than just a challenge – it was an obsession (Salkeld, 1993). His decision to push for the summit with the inexperienced Irvine, instead of the more seasoned climber Noel Odell, raises questions about his mindset in those final days. Did he knowingly take an extreme risk to fulfill what had become a personal crusade?

Mallory and Irvine's climb is often compared to later successful ascents, particularly the 1953 expedition of Edmund Hillary and Tenzing Norgay. The differences between these two attempts illustrate the evolution of high-altitude mountaineering and highlight the nearly insurmountable odds that Mallory and Irvine faced. The route taken by Hillary and Norgay via the South Col was far more logistically feasible than the Northeast Ridge attempted by Mallory and Irvine. The South Col route, first scouted in 1951, provided a more direct approach, with fewer technical obstacles and more opportunities to establish supply camps. By contrast, the Northeast Ridge presented significant challenges, particularly the Second Step, a near-vertical rock face at 28,250 feet. Modern climbers rely on a fixed ladder to ascend this section, and many experts believe that without contemporary climbing techniques and equipment, Mallory and Irvine would have been unable to scale it. If they did manage to climb it, the effort required would have left them dangerously exhausted for the final push to the summit.

In addition to logistical advantages, Hillary and Norgay benefited from decades of technological advancements. Their clothing, boots, and insulated gear provided far greater protection against the elements. Their oxygen systems were vastly superior to those used in 1924, allowing for sustained physical effort at extreme altitudes. Their ascent was also meticulously planned, with multiple summit attempts built into the strategy, ensuring that every factor was optimized for success. When contrasted with Mallory and Irvine's expedition – marked by rudimentary equipment, unpredictable weather, and a reliance on sheer endurance – their odds of success seem almost insurmountable (Salkeld, 1996).

The discovery of Mallory's body in 1999 provided the most tangible evidence yet of what may have happened to the climbers. His remains, found on the North Face at approximately 26,760 feet, suggested that he suffered a catastrophic fall. His injuries, particularly the broken leg and deep rope abrasions around his torso, indicated that he and Irvine were likely roped together when the accident occurred. The condition of his body, with the puncture wound on his forehead, further suggested that he may have struck his head on a rock or been hit by his falling ice axe, rendering him unconscious or fatally injured before coming to rest on the mountainside. His position, facing uphill, indicated that he was still attempting to arrest his fall even in his final moments.

One of the most intriguing aspects of the 1999 discovery was the absence of key artifacts. The Kodak Vest Pocket camera, which Irvine was believed to have been carrying, was nowhere to be found. If recovered and intact, this camera could potentially provide photographic evidence of whether Mallory and Irvine reached the summit before their deaths. However, given the extreme conditions on Everest, the likelihood of any surviving images remains uncertain. Similarly, the photograph of Ruth Mallory that George had promised to leave on the summit was missing, leading some to speculate that he may have successfully reached the top and placed it there before descending. Others argue that the photo could have been lost during the fall or disintegrated over time.

Despite these compelling clues, the mystery of their fate remains unresolved. The discovery of Irvine's ice axe in 1933, found roughly 200 yards east of the First Step, initially suggested that he had fallen separately from Mallory, possibly continuing his descent alone. However, this theory has been complicated by the 2024 discovery of what is believed to be Irvine's foot in the Central Rongbuk Glacier, found by a team led by Jimmy Chin. This find suggests that Irvine's body may have traveled considerable distances over the past century due to the movement of the glacier. The presence of the foot, still clad in a boot bearing Irvine's name tag, raises the possibility that the rest of his body – and potentially the missing camera – could still be nearby, waiting to be uncovered.

While Mallory and Irvine's climb has been extensively analyzed, their role in Everest's broader history is often underappreciated. Their attempt in 1924 represented a bridge between two eras of mountaineering – the age of exploration and the age of scientific expeditions. Prior to their attempt, Everest was viewed largely as an insurmountable peak, a place where human endurance was tested against the most extreme conditions on Earth. Their climb demonstrated that a summit attempt was not only possible but that success was within reach, setting the stage for future expeditions. Their disappearance, rather than deterring climbers, only fueled further attempts to conquer Everest, leading to renewed efforts in the 1930s and ultimately culminating in the successful ascent by Hillary and Norgay in 1953.

Mallory and Irvine's legacy is also reflected in how modern climbers measure their own achievements. The question of whether they reached the summit has become a point of philosophical debate, with some arguing that the true measure of success is not just reaching the top but returning safely. John Mallory, George Mallory's son, famously stated, "To me, the only way you achieve a summit is to come back alive; the job's half done if you don't get down again." This perspective underscores the shift in mountaineering culture from the romanticized, almost reckless ambition of the early 20th century to the more calculated and strategic mindset of modern climbers.

Yet, despite this shift, the allure of Mallory and Irvine's final climb remains as strong as ever. Their names are invoked not just in discussions of Everest but in broader conversations about human ambition, risk, and the limits of endurance. Their story continues to inspire climbers who see themselves as part of a long tradition of explorers pushing the boundaries of what is possible. Even as Everest has become increasingly commercialized, with guided expeditions and modern technology making the climb more accessible than ever before, the mystery of 1924 serves as a reminder of a time when the mountain was an uncharted frontier, and those who dared to climb it were venturing into the unknown.

The mystery of whether Mallory and Irvine reached the summit of Mount Everest before perishing has remained one of the most captivating and debated questions in the history of exploration. The absence of definitive proof – most notably the missing Kodak Vest Pocket camera that Irvine was believed to have been carrying – ensures that their final moments will remain a subject of speculation and fascination. The 1999 discovery of Mallory's body provided significant clues, but in many ways, it only deepened the enigma. Without photographic evidence, the question of whether they stood atop Everest before their deaths lingers unanswered, and it is possible that it always will.

The search for Irvine's camera has become a quest in its own right, with multiple expeditions dedicated to locating his remains in the hopes of recovering the device. If found, and if the film were miraculously intact, it could provide irrefutable evidence of whether Mallory and Irvine summited Everest nearly three decades before Hillary and Norgay. However, the extreme conditions on Everest – subzero temperatures, high winds, and exposure to moisture – make it unlikely that any film inside the camera would be salvageable after a century. Even if the camera were to be found, there is no guarantee that it would hold the long-sought answers.

Yet, for many, the absence of definitive proof is what makes their story so compelling. If their success or failure were conclusively determined, it might diminish the legend surrounding them. Their disappearance has allowed each generation to project its own values and aspirations onto their climb, transforming them into symbols of human ambition, perseverance, and sacrifice. This is one of the reasons why Mallory and Irvine's story continues to resonate so powerfully, not just within the mountaineering community but across popular culture as well.

Their climb and mysterious fate have inspired numerous books, documentaries, and fictionalized accounts that explore the human drive to conquer the unknown. Holzel & Salkeld (1999) extensively examined the evidence surrounding their expedition, piecing together the clues left behind. Wade Davis's *Into the Silence* (2012) provided a broader historical context, examining the psychological and societal impact of World War I on the men who attempted Everest in the early 20th century. The novel *Paths of Glory* by Jeffrey Archer fictionalized their story, presenting a dramatized interpretation of their final moments on the mountain. These works, along with countless articles, research papers, and personal memoirs from climbers and historians, reflect the enduring fascination with Mallory and Irvine's climb.

Film and television have also played a significant role in keeping their story alive. *The Wildest Dream* (2010), featuring Conrad Anker, retraced Mallory's final climb, blending historical footage with modern reenactments. National Geographic and the BBC have produced several documentaries exploring their journey, highlighting the advancements in mountaineering that their expedition helped inspire. These portrayals continue to shape public perception, reinforcing the narrative of Mallory and Irvine as heroic, tragic figures lost to the pursuit of greatness.

The debate surrounding Mallory and Irvine's climb also raises broader questions about the cost of exploration and the fine line between ambition and recklessness. History is filled with figures who ventured into the unknown and never returned – Sir John Franklin's doomed Arctic expedition, Robert Falcon Scott's tragic Antarctic journey, and Amelia Earhart's disappearance over the Pacific all share thematic similarities with the story of Mallory and Irvine. In each case, the absence of definitive answers has contributed to their mythic status, transforming them from explorers into legends.

Mountaineering, by its nature, has always blurred the boundary between calculated risk and dangerous obsession. Mallory, in particular, was known for his deep and relentless fixation on Everest. Some have suggested that he exhibited early signs of what is now referred to as summit fever – the overwhelming drive to reach the top at all costs, often leading climbers to ignore the dangers that could prevent them from returning safely (Salkeld, 1993). His repeated attempts to summit Everest, despite the mounting risks, speak to his singular determination, a quality that has been both admired and criticized in later analyses of his expedition.

The tragedy of Mallory and Irvine also raises questions about the societal impact of high-risk exploration. The pursuit of "firsts" – whether it be reaching the highest peak, crossing the poles, or venturing into space – often comes at a great cost. The deaths of explorers are mourned, but their sacrifices are also used to inspire future generations. This duality – of loss and legacy – is central to the way Mallory and Irvine are remembered. Their disappearance added to the mystique of Everest itself, turning it into a symbol of human perseverance and the ultimate challenge for climbers.

Modern Everest expeditions have been shaped in part by the lessons of past tragedies, including that of 1924. The commercialization of the mountain, with guided expeditions and fixed ropes making the ascent more accessible, has fundamentally altered the nature of climbing Everest. Some argue that this has diminished the spirit of adventure that defined early attempts, turning the mountain into a tourist destination rather than a place of genuine exploration. Others point out that modern safety measures, while reducing the risk, have not eliminated it – deaths still occur on Everest each year, and climbers continue to push their limits in pursuit of personal achievement.

The ultimate question remains: will we ever truly know if Mallory and Irvine reached the summit? The recent discovery of what is believed to be Irvine's remains has renewed interest in finding further evidence, but Everest remains a vast and unpredictable environment. Even if new discoveries are made, they may not provide a definitive answer. And even if they did, would it change the way we perceive their climb?

Some argue that the uncertainty is what keeps their legend alive. The idea that they may have stood atop the world's highest peak before vanishing into history adds to the mystique of their story. In this sense, the myth of Mallory and Irvine is just as powerful as the truth. Whether they reached the summit or not, their journey embodies the essence of exploration – an unwavering pursuit of the unknown, driven by the belief that some challenges are worth facing simply "because they are there."

References

Chapters 2, 3, and 4

- Bruce, C. G. (1934). *The Assault on Mount Everest, 1922*. London: Edward Arnold & Co.
- Mason, K. (1955). *Abode of Snow: A History of Himalayan Exploration and Mountaineering*. London: Rupert Hart-Davis.
- Norton, H. (1952). *The Fight for Everest: 1924*. London: Edward Arnold.
- Brown, T. (2023). *Mallory and His Pursuits*. Oxford University Press.
- Davies, L. (2020). *Everest's Early Explorers*. Cambridge University Press.
- Evans, R. (2021). *The Life and Times of George Mallory*. Yale University Press.
- Foster, M. (2021). *Letters from the Alpine Club*. HarperCollins.
- Gray, N. (2019). *Into the Himalayas: The British Ascents of Everest*. Random House.
- Jameson, P. (2022). *Charterhouse and the Making of Mallory*. Penguin Books.
- Johnson, D. (2022). *Mountaineers and Minds*. Routledge.
- Jones, A. (2018). *Surrey's Histories and Homes*. Vintage Books.
- Lee, K. (2021). *Mallory at Charterhouse: A Journey Interrupted*. Simon & Schuster.
- Lee, K. (2022). *From England to Everest*. Macmillan.

- Morris, G., & Wilson, T. (2021). *The Mount Everest Committee: Origins and Ambitions.* Bloomsbury.
- Parker, J. (2023). *Adventures and Alliances in the Age of Exploration.* Basic Books.
- Roberts, H. (2019). *The Legacy of Mallory.* Princeton University Press.
- Smith, C. (2020). *Godalming: A Cultural History.* Oxford University Press.
- Thompson, B. (2021). *Reconnaissance of the Roof of the World.* Verso.
- Turner, F. (2023). *The Great Expedition to Everest.* Harper & Row.
- Wilson, L., & Younghusband, F. (2021). *The Royal Geographical Society and Its Explorers.* Cambridge University Press.
- Young, G., & Wilson, H. (2022). *Friends on the Frontier: Mallory and Young's Adventures.* University of Chicago Press.

Online Sources:

- *Mallory at War* - http://thegeorgemalloryfoundation.org/mallory-at-war
- *The Woman Behind George Mallory's Everest Dream* - https://www.telegraph.co.uk/travel/news/woman-behind-george-mallory-everest/

Chapters 4 and 1922 Expedition References

- Davis, L. (2020). *Everest's Early Explorers.* Cambridge University Press.
- Evans, R. (2021). *The Life and Times of George Mallory.* Yale University Press.
- Gray, N. (2019). *Into the Himalayas: The British Ascents of Everest.* Random House.
- Johnson, D. (2022). *Mountaineers and Minds.* Routledge.

- Parker, J. (2023). *Adventures and Alliances in the Age of Exploration.* Basic Books.
- Roberts, H. (2019). *The Legacy of Mallory.* Princeton University Press.
- Brown, T. (2021). *High Altitudes: Early Climbs on Everest.* Oxford University Press.
- Davis, A. (2020). *Pathfinders on Everest: The 1922 British Expedition.* Cambridge University Press.
- Evans, R. (2019). *Mountaineering in the Himalayas: A History of Early Expeditions.* Yale University Press.
- Johnson, M. (2022). *The Physiology of High-Altitude Climbing.* Princeton University Press.
- Jones, L. (2020). *Everest's Early Pioneers.* Harvard University Press.
- Smith, P. (2021). *Mountaineering and Modern Science.* Stanford University Press.
- Taylor, J. (2021). *Photography on Everest: Documenting Exploration and Tragedy.* University of Chicago Press.
- Williams, B. (2019). *The Summit Pursuit: Early Everest Expeditions.* Columbia University Press.

Online Sources:

- Mallory's 1922 Letter to Ruth - https://magdalene.maxarchiveservices.co.uk/index.php/to-ruth-mallory-june-1922-avalanche-full-transcript;isad?sf_culture=pt

Mallory and 1923 Speaking Tour

- Conefrey, M. *Fallen: George Mallory and the Tragic 1924 Everest Expedition.*

Online Sources:

- https://www.himalayana.com/1923-mallory-in-america/

Mallory Letters and Obituaries
Online Sources:

- https://magdalene.maxarchiveservices.co.uk/index.php/correspondence-2
- https://www.himalayanclub.org/hj/13/11/in-memoriam-26/

Chapters 6, 7, and 8

- Davis, L. (2020). *Everest's Early Explorers*. Cambridge University Press.

Online Sources:

- https://itisalwayssunrisesomewhere.wordpress.com/2013/01/29/george-mallory-the-dreamer/
- *Low Barometric Pressure Study* - https://rmets.onlinelibrary.wiley.com/doi/10.1002/wea.590
- *1999 Expedition Report* - https://www.mountainzone.com/everest/99/north/disp5-4dave2.html
- Breashears, D., & Salkeld, A. (1999). *Last Climb: The Legendary Everest Expeditions of George Mallory*. National Geographic.

Chapter 9 - The Search for Andrew Irvine
Online Sources:

- https://www.dailymail.co.uk/news/article-13949875/Inside-tragic-final-days-Everest-climber-Andrew-Sandy-Irvine-partial-remains-discovered.html
- https://www.bbc.com/news/articles/cy0g2p47xd5o
- https://www.dw.com/en/mount-everest-the-100-year-old-mystery-of-mallory-and-irvine/a-70524517

Chapter 10 - The Legacy of Mallory and Irvine
Online Sources:

- https://www.himalayanclub.org/hj/18/1/everest-1953-1/
- https://www.theguardian.com/world/1953/jun/02/everest.nepal
- https://nzhistory.govt.nz/edmund-hillary-and-tensing-norgay-reach-summit-of-everest
- https://everest70.com/the-expedition-team-1953/#

www.ingramcontent.com/pod-product-compliance
Lightning Source LLC
LaVergne TN
LVHW021958060526
838201LV00048B/1613